OVID
Myth and Metamorphosis

ANCIENTS IN ACTION

Also available

Catullus
Amanda Kolson Hurley

Horace
Philip D. Hills

Lucretius
John Godwin

Ovid: Love Songs
Genevieve Liveley

Spartacus
Theresa Urbainczyk

ANCIENTS IN ACTION

OVID
Myth and Metamorphosis

Sarah Annes Brown

BRISTOL CLASSICAL PRESS

First published in 2005 by
Bristol Classical Press, an imprint of
Gerald Duckworth & Co. Ltd.
90-93 Cowcross Street, London EC1M 6BF
Tel: 020 7490 7300
Fax: 020 7490 0080
inquiries@duckworth-publishers.co.uk
www.ducknet.co.uk

© 2005 by Sarah Annes Brown

All rights reserved. No part of this publication
may be reproduced, stored in a retrieval system, or
transmitted, in any form or by any means, electronic,
mechanical, photocopying, recording or otherwise,
without the prior permission of the publisher.

A catalogue record for this book is available
from the British Library

ISBN 1 85399 672 6

The author and publisher are grateful for permission to reproduce copyright material from the following works:
'If you will let me sing' by HD (Hilda Doolittle), from *Collected Poems, 1912-1944*, copyright 1982 by The Estate of Hilda Doolittle. Used by permission of New Directions Publishing Corporation.
Excerpts from *Tales from Ovid* by Ted Hughes, *After Ovid* by Michael Hofmann and James Lasdun, and *Collected Poems* by Sylvia Plath. Used by permission of Faber & Faber.
'Science' copyright 1925, 1929 and renewed 1953, 1957 by Robinson Jeffers, from *Selected Poetry of Robinson Jeffers*. Used by permission of Random House, Inc.
The Metamorphoses of Ovid, translated by David R. Slavitt, copyright 1994 by David R. Slavitt. Used by permission of The Johns Hopkins University Press.
Excerpt from 'Where I Live in This Honorable House of the Laurel Tree' from *To Bedlam and Part Way Back* by Anne Sexton, copyright 1960 by Anne Sexton, renewed 1988 by Linda G. Sexton. Used by permission of Houghton Mifflin Company. All rights reserved.
Excerpt from 'Tongues' from *Red Under the Skin* by Natasha Sajé, copyright 1994. Reprinted by permission of the University of Pittsburgh Press.
'Metamorphoses' by C.H. Sisson, from *Collected Poems*, 1984. Used by permission of Carcanet Press.

Contents

Preface	7
Introduction	9
1. Daphne	45
2. Actaeon	67
3. Philomela	85
4. Arachne	105
5. Pygmalion	123
6. Ovid in the Third Millennium	143
Note on Translations	147
Further Reading	149
Works Cited and Consulted	151
Index	155

For Alex

Preface

This short introduction to Ovid's masterpiece, the *Metamorphoses*, is aimed at anyone who wants to find out more about the poem and its impact on Western culture: general readers, students in the humanities, even fully-fledged classicists.

Considering the centuries which have passed since it was written – Ovid died nearly two thousand years ago – the *Metamorphoses* is a surprisingly accessible text. The stories Ovid tells are astonishingly varied – birth, death, creation, war, flood, famine, rape and romance all compete for our attention.

This book begins with an introduction which identifies and describes the *Metamorphoses*' most notable features – such as its presentation of the gods and its treatment of metamorphosis itself – and places the poem within Ovid's own cultural context: the age of Augustus. Each of the following five chapters is devoted to a single myth. Here I explore the impact these tales have had on later writers, artists and film makers and analyse the relationship between the developing creative reception of the *Metamorphoses* and the many cultural shifts which have taken place since Ovid's own day.

Although there were many candidates for inclusion – Icarus, Ceyx and Alcyone, Narcissus and Callisto are just a few examples of other Ovidian stories which repay close attention – the five myths I eventually chose are all strikingly memorable and have been adapted and interpreted in countless different ways.

Apollo's unrequited love for Daphne is the first of Ovid's

many troubling rape narratives and may make uneasy reading for today's readers of the *Metamorphoses*. The story of Actaeon, whose punishment seems so disproportionate to his crime, has a haunting, mysterious quality not unlike that of Coleridge's 'Rime of the Ancient Mariner' – both centre on men who break a strange taboo. The tale of Philomela and Procne is one of the most shocking in the poem, and I offer a fresh interpretation of this violent narrative, a controversial reading which is derived from my earlier research into literary depictions of the sister relationship. The fourth and fifth chapters are devoted to Arachne and Pygmalion, two of Ovid's many striking artist figures. But whereas Arachne the weaver is punished for daring to compete with the goddess Athena, the sculptor Pygmalion is granted his heart's desire through the miraculous intervention of Venus.

Introduction

I was introduced to Ovid by an unsuitable boyfriend in the summer of 1989. As far as Ovid goes I've never looked back – though the boyfriend has long since been replaced. This book is a short introduction to his best-known poem, the *Metamorphoses*. I hope to show that Ovid is still a hugely important and influential force in Western culture, not a recherché figure of interest only to classicists and academics. Much of this book is focused on the *reception* of the *Metamorphoses*, in other words, on the way it has influenced later works – whether poems, paintings, novels or films. Many of the best known productions of Western culture – including works by Dante, Chaucer, Shakespeare, Goethe and Proust – are indebted to this poem.

Although the *Metamorphoses* begins with the creation of the world and ends with the apotheosis of Julius Caesar, the intervening books do not comprise an orderly account of Greco-Roman myth and history. Some very rough trends can be identified – towards the end of the poem the focus moves westward, from Greece to Rome, as Ovid first retells the story of Rome's founder, Aeneas, and then relates a handful of legends – that of Pomona and Vertumnus for example – which are Roman rather than Greek. But it is difficult to map any orderly scheme – whether narrative, thematic or contextual – on to the poem. Or rather, it is too easy – any number of competing explanations have been provided by the poem's many commentators. Some are more convincing than others, but collectively they suggest that no single explanation can do justice to the poem's complexity. Each generation, each individual reader, will tend to concentrate on certain stories, themes and threads and disregard others. Seeing the *Metamorphoses* all in one go is rather like trying to see a free-standing statue all at once – we can only really concentrate on one angle, a few details, at a time. The same is of course true of other complex literary works – *Hamlet* is a good example.

Anyone who turns to the *Metamorphoses* is likely to have quite a wide frame of cultural reference to draw on already, much of it derived, whether directly or indirectly, from Ovid himself. Reading the story of Orpheus and Eurydice, for example, will be a slightly different experience if we already know Offenbach's *Orpheus in the Underworld*, Cocteau's *Orphée* or Rushdie's *The Ground Beneath Her Feet*. The impossibility of reading Ovid pristinely, as it were, is nicely suggested by Ted Hughes in his translation of 'Pyramus and Thisbe'. This story of star-crossed lovers is already familiar to nearly all first time English-speaking readers of Ovid through its comic re-enactment in *A Midsummer Night's Dream*. In *Tales from Ovid*, Thisbe seems to escape from her Ovidian setting in order to remind us that she is now part of a larger, post-classical, literary landscape. She and Pyramus arrange to meet:

> Their rendezvous the mulberry tree
> Over the tomb of Ninus, *a famous landmark* [my italics]

The last phrase is not in Ovid; we may infer that the 'landmark' is literary as well as geographical, 'famous' because it is immortalised as 'Ninny's tomb' by Shakespeare's Francis Flute, the bellows-mender. In other words Hughes' Thisbe seems to be aware that her readers already know her story.

Introduction

But Ovid's influence went beyond putting dozens of stories into the literary domain – the *way* he told these stories also had a huge impact on later literature. When we begin to pick up on Ovid's peculiar narrative style, his insistent reminders that we are only reading a fiction, we are likely to make connections with other equally self-conscious productions. We might think of Lawrence Sterne's *Tristram Shandy*, and the various games it plays with its readers, or of the post-modern stories of Jorge Luis Borges. But we might just as easily be put in mind of the *Simpsons* episode ('Treehouse of Horror IX') in which Bart and Lisa are sucked into their TV set and become part of a further inset cartoon programme, 'The Itchy and Scratchy Show'.

Ovid's original audience would obviously have made completely different connections – with the earlier presentation of Orpheus in Virgil's *Georgics*, perhaps, or with works by the similarly mannered 'neoterics' (new poets) such as Catullus. Although we can begin to reconstruct the literary and cultural context which gave birth to the *Metamorphoses*, we can never completely reproduce the experience of the poem's first readers. Many of Ovid's most important literary influences no longer exist – we know of some through brief quotation or report in the works of others, but he probably drew on other sources which have vanished without trace. Even though the *Metamorphoses* has come down to us intact, it is not precisely the same poem Ovid wrote because the audience he wrote for, the cultural moment he wrote in, have vanished. But it doesn't matter that our Ovid is a twenty-first century Ovid rather than the original model. The works of any really influential writer – for example Shakespeare – are endlessly reinvented, whether it is the text itself which is altered – the science fiction film version of *The Tempest*,

Ovid

Forbidden Planet, is a memorable example – or simply the perspective from which it is viewed. Whether we try to reconstruct a Roman reading of Ovid or are relaxed about reading his works from a modern perspective we shouldn't forget all the intervening 'Ovids' which the last two millennia have thrown up.

The medieval commentary tradition was particularly important. Clerics would adapt classical texts such as the attractive but reprehensible *Metamorphoses*, making the stories palatable by relating them to Christian doctrine. Best known of these commentaries is the fourteenth-century *Ovide moralisé* of Pierre Bersuire. The very strangeness and (to modern eyes) inaptness of some of the moralisers' interpretations – the association forged between Myrrha (who slept with her father) and the Virgin Mary for example – make them paradoxically Ovidian. This simultaneous rejection and embrace of Ovid is neatly suggested by the twelfth-century Cistercian abbot, Bernard of Clairvaux, when he condemns the fashion for portraying metamorphic compound creatures in church carvings. 'What is the point of such ridiculous monstrosity, the strange kind of shapeless shapeliness, of shapely shapelessness', he rails (Barnard, 60). But the chiming repetition here surely recalls one of Ovid's most famous lines – apparently one of his three personal favourites – his description of the minotaur as a 'semibovemque virum semivirumque bovem', 'the man half-bull and the bull half-man' (*Art of Love* 2.24).

Influences

Even though we cannot turn back the clock and read the poem exactly as Ovid's first readers would have done, we can piece together quite a lot of information about the forces –

Introduction

literary, historical and biographical – which shaped the *Metamorphoses*. Ovid himself – or Publius Ovidius Naso to give him his full name – was born in Sulmo in 43 BC to parents of equestrian rank, the Roman 'gentry' class. He moved to Rome and became a prominent poet, although in AD 7, as he was completing the *Metamorphoses*, his successful career was cut short when the Emperor Augustus banished him to Tomis in modern Romania. It is unclear exactly what Ovid did to alienate Augustus. In his exile poetry the poet suggests two reasons: first, his racy *Art of Love* in which he advised young men (and young women) how to succeed with the opposite sex, secondly a mysterious 'error' – perhaps the inadvertent discovery of an imperial scandal.

Ovid's nemesis, Augustus, was the adopted son of Julius Caesar and one of the most celebrated Roman emperors. Although his achievements were immense his methods were often ruthless, and his ambition to restore the virtues of the more austere Republican era – the good old Roman values of discipline, obedience, morality and a strong commitment to the family as an institution – compromised political enquiry and free expression. An obvious modern comparison is Margaret Thatcher's call for a return to 'Victorian Values'. In Paul West's contribution to Philip Terry's anthology *Ovid Metamorphosed* (2001), a short story called 'Nightfall on the Romanian Coast', a different parallel is drawn by the ghost of the long dead Ovid:

> My own view, though, is that I was sent packing for being unfaithful to poetry, for not writing the wholesome stuff the Emperor wanted; as the Boss, he owned all that was thought, said or done. To put it in Soviet terms, I had refused to come up with tractor poems, paeans to hydroelectric stations, to the

Ovid

founders of the party, to the rustic rabble and the proles of Rome.

The generation which immediately preceded Ovid provided him with some powerful – perhaps oppressive – role models. Lucretius, Virgil and Horace were the most famous writers of this slightly older generation, though more important models for the *Metamorphoses* itself can be found in the works of still earlier writers; the catalogue poems of Hellenistic Greek writers were a particularly strong influence. The Hellenistic age lasted from the end of the fourth century BC to the end of the first century BC. Its literature has traditionally been seen as secondary to the productions of the earlier 'classical' period. One of these Hellenistic writers was Callimachus, a Greek poet and scholar of the third century BC. His *Aitia* – 'causes' – in many ways looks forward to Ovid's poem, as it explains the mythical origins of numerous Greek customs in a witty and sophisticated way. (A more familiar and more recent example of an aetiological collection is Rudyard Kipling's *Just So Stories*.) Another poem which undoubtedly influenced Ovid was Nicander of Colophon's *Heteroeumena*, a mythological epic, though this has not survived.

Genre

The *Metamorphoses* is a story collection. Over the course of fifteen books (some 12,000 lines in total) Ovid tells hundreds of stories. Some – those of Pygmalion or Ceyx and Alcyone – are told at great length, whereas others are rather allusions than stories, brief references to tales the reader is assumed to know already. Although, generically, the *Metamorphoses* can be linked with earlier Hellenistic catalogue poems, it is an exceptionally

Introduction

hard work to classify. It is written in the metre of epic (the hexameter, in which every line consists of six metrical feet), yet it embraces a range of genres including tragedy, comedy, panegyric, history, philosophy and love poetry. Indeed one of its distinctive features is its ability to slide from one mode into another. When Ovid (rather briefly) retells the already canonical *Aeneid* towards the end of the *Metamorphoses* the narrator slips in and out of the expected epic and heroic mode to indulge in episodes of pastoral and love elegy. The poem thus enacts as well as describes metamorphosis. In so far as the *Metamorphoses* is an epic – and a lot of ink has been expended debating that question – it is a kind of *über*-epic. Most epics chart a single military campaign or heroic quest, but the *Metamorphoses*' subject matter is life, the universe and everything: its starting point predates the creation of the world and it concludes in Ovid's own Augustan age.

Metamorphosis

In some of the stories Ovid tells (Narcissus' metamorphosis into a flower is a case in point) the transformation seems tacked on as an afterthought; however the phenomenon of metamorphosis is far more than simply a convenient umbrella concept for yet another mythological catalogue poem. Ovid is intensely interested in exactly what happens when his characters – whether hapless victims or triumphant gods – undergo a transformation; how does it feel to be changed into an entirely different form? In different stories metamorphosis provides an escape route, a punishment, a reward, or simply closure. Although generally there is a downwards momentum – from a human into an animal or flower – sometimes the trajectory is upward, as when Pyrrha and Deucalion create a new race of men from the stones they throw behind them after the flood, or Hercules becomes a god. Often a person's new state is a crystallisation of his or her strongest character trait – savage, cannibalistic King Lycaon changes into a wolf; hard-hearted Anaxarete is turned to stone. But sometimes the connection is more obscure, and needs to be explained to the reader. Warlike Tereus is transformed into a hoopoe because the crest and long beak of that bird suggest the helmet and sword of a soldier ready for battle.

So metamorphic is Ovid's imagination that he seems to hint at transformation even when none has taken place. In the shifting Ovidian world we feel that anyone – or anything – might be on the verge of changing shape. At the death of Orpheus, for example, the rivers and trees are simultaneously inhuman and human in their response (11.46-8):

> The trees shed their leaves as though they were tearing out their hair, and they say that the rivers were swollen with their own tears.

Conversely, when Alcyone is told that her husband has to go on a dangerous voyage the description of her shock and grief hints at various metamorphoses which never quite advance from metaphor (11.416-19):

> Alcyone immediately felt a chill in the very marrow of her bones, her face was as pale as boxwood, and her cheeks were wet with streaming tears. Three times she tried to speak, three times her face was watered with tears.

Her inability to speak is itself a key symptom of metamorphosis in Ovid, though here it is caused by grief alone. Elsewhere such

Introduction

a hint at the loss of human form or capacity is the prelude to full-blown metamorphosis. When the Bacchantes who killed Orpheus are changed into trees Ovid concludes: 'you might think her knotty arms were real branches, and if you thought so you would not be mistaken' (11.82-3).

Metamorphosis is more than a repeated event in the poem – it is part of its linguistic texture. Words shift their meaning, through either a change in their form or a change in their context. Although Echo can only repeat the words of others she subtly transforms them. Narcissus angrily rejects her, crying 'May I die before I give you power over me', to which she replies 'I give you power over me' (3.391-2). Sometimes, like one of his characters mid-metamorphosis, Ovid's words possess two meanings simultaneously. As Myrrha is transformed into a tree we are told that her *medulla* remained the same. This is true only at the linguistic level. Although Myrrha's body has been completely metamorphosed, a double meaning – *medulla* may mean either pith or marrow – suggests otherwise. Here, as elsewhere, the narrator seems to play with the reading habits we have picked up as we progress through the poem. Generally when Ovid tells us that something remains the same after metamorphosis – the shining beauty of Daphne for example – he refers to some real, physical vestige of the old self, not an accident of language.

Similar wordplay seems to be at work in the tale of Byblis, victim of an incestuous passion for her brother. She takes up her pen to reveal the terrible secret to him in a letter. The word used for pen is *ferrum* – this can signify any sharp metal object but its most common meaning is 'sword'. (Her writing surface is a wax tablet rather than paper.) If we first interpret *ferrum* as sword, we may not simply be misreading. Her name resembles the Greek *biblos*, a written document, and in carving her confessional letter she seals her own doom as surely as though she had stabbed herself.

Boundaries

Ovid's fascination with metamorphosis and wordplay is matched by his absorption in other borderline states, and his fondness for blurring boundaries of all kinds. Some of his characters are doomed when they cross very literal boundaries to step on tabooed territory. Others step over metaphorical boundaries – as when Myrrha's admirable love for her father develops into outlawed lust. Ovid himself, as well as his characters, has a fondness for transgression. Apparently secure historical boundaries, for example, are put under pressure by the poem's narrator. At first his account of the earth's development seems ordered and sequential. We learn how the Edenic golden age gave way to the less favourable silver and bronze ages, before declining further into the iron age. But this apparently logical deterioration is problematised by the way Ovid describes the last age, that of iron (1.138-42):

> Men went right into the bowels of the earth, and the treasure which had been hidden in the Stygian shades was dug up – the wealth that incites men to crime. Soon came baneful *iron*, and then *gold*, more baneful still ... [my italics].

There does not at first seem to be anything odd in this little morality fable explaining that money is the root of all evil. But when we are first told that iron is mined we connect this innovation with the fact that this is the 'iron age', and thus may feel wrong-footed when we learn that gold too is mined. Is some connection with the long distant 'golden age' being hinted at?

Introduction

It is curious that the basest and latest age should be so bound up with the substance associated with man's perfect original state. This apparent disjuncture may reflect the fact that Ovid was supposedly living in a second Golden Age – that of Augustus. By blurring the boundary between the iron and golden ages Ovid seems to undercut the pretensions of his own time to be called golden, perhaps hinting that it is 'golden' only in an economic rather than a moral or cultural sense. Such a view is more clearly and cynically articulated in the *Art of Love* when he describes women's fondness for costly gifts (2.277-8):

> This is truly a golden age; many an honour is sold for gold, and gold procures love.

Spatial and geographical boundaries, as well as temporal ones, are subject to confusion in the poem. Two memorable passages, from Book 1 and Book 15 respectively, describe (in very different contexts) the processes of flux and reversal. In the first, the flood sent by Jupiter to punish mankind results in a weirdly topsy-turvy landscape, surreal and strangely beautiful (1.297-303):

> And sometimes it happened that an anchor was embedded in a green meadow, or curved keels brushed over the vineyards. And where slender goats had once grazed, now the ugly sea cows rested their bulk. The Nereids wonder at the underwater houses, towns and groves, dolphins take over the woods and swim among the high branches, shaking the oak trees when they crash into them.

In the second passage, which is part of a long monologue spoken by the Greek polymath Pythagoras, we learn of a far slower process

Ovid

of reversal, one which is more unsettling because it is based on historical fact rather than mythological fancy (15.259-65):

'I don't believe anything stays the same for long. Thus the Golden Age gave way to the Iron Age, and places have changed their state just as often. I myself have seen dry land change to sea, and I've seen land emerge from the water. Seashells lie far from the shore, and a rusty anchor has been discovered at the top of a mountain.'

In fact yet another of the many boundaries Ovid plays with is that between reality and fiction. We may dismiss the flood of Book 1 as a fable, only to reflect that geological proof exists for equally dramatic shifts, albeit over a longer timescale.

Pythagoras

The speech of Pythagoras takes up nearly half of Book 15; although the last portion of his speech is a lecture on mutability, the first part is devoted to an attack on meat eating. He describes the fate of slaughtered animals very feelingly (15.133-5):

A victim sees the grain he helped to cultivate sprinkled on his brow. Then he is struck down, and the knife – which he might already have noticed reflected in the bright water – is stained with his blood.

Although some of the poem's readers have added Ovid to the list of famous historical vegetarians on the strength of this passage, others have detected a satirical note in the polemic, and have felt that the entire speech is undermined by the philosopher's mili-

Introduction

tant vegetarianism. Generally the tone and overall significance of Pythagoras' speech is difficult to gauge. For example, who is being satirised here: the speaker or the poets he dismisses? (15.153-5):

> O mortals, stupefied by your dread of icy death, why do you fear the Styx, the shades, and empty names? They are poets' fancies, bugbears from an invented world.

Whether we read it straight or conclude that Ovid was sending Pythagoras up, it is probably fair to say that the interest of modern readers is sparked far less readily by this long speech than by the lively tales themselves.

Race

One further boundary, one to which Ovid was not conspicuously alert but yet which colours the poem's reception, is that of race. In a poem whose human characters liaise with trees, clouds, statues, their immediate kin and farmyard animals, it is hardly surprising that no one bats an eyelid when Greek Perseus marries Ethiopian Andromeda, and Dido's unsuitability as a wife for Aeneas has nothing to do with the fact that she's an African (from Libya). But despite the poem's apparent colour-blindness, some of Ovid's imitators have used his adaptable tales to engage with issues of race. In a poem included by Hofmann and Lasdun in *After Ovid*, Fred D'Aguiar's retelling of Pyramus and Thisbe, the young lovers are separated by a colour bar:

> I am black and you're white:
> What's the day without night
> To measure it by and give

Ovid

It definition; life.
We'll go where love's colour-
Blind and therefore coloured.

The move is a fairly obvious one – a similar impulse led to the Capulets and Montagues being recast as the white Jets and Puerto Rican Sharks in *West Side Story* – but dovetails nicely with the tale's slightly unusual final metamorphosis. Pyramus and Thisbe retain their human forms, but the mulberry changes colour (from white to red) when Pyramus' blood falls on it.

We might expect race to bring a new charge to twentieth-century retellings of Ovid, but not, perhaps, to eighteenth-century translations into heroic couplets, such as this extract from the story of Niobe, whose children were all killed by the gods:

> One only daughter lives, and she the least;
> The queen close clasp'd the daughter to her breast:
> 'Ye heav'nly pow'rs, ah spare me one,' she cry'd,
> 'Ah! spare me one,' the vocal hills reply'd:
> In vain she begs, the Fates her suit deny,
> In her embrace she sees her daughter die.

But we may respond rather differently to this account of an anguished mother, cruelly deprived of all her children, once we know that the poet, Phillis Wheatley, was taken from the Gambia to Boston as a slave. As well as having experienced the loss of her own family as a child, Wheatley would have been aware that the children of slaves were routinely sold to other masters and never seen again, and wondered, like Niobe, 'why is such privilege to them allowed?'

In another story from Philip Terry's *Ovid Metamorphosed*,

Introduction

Rosalind Belben's 'Disjecta Membra', Ovid seduces his mistress' slave girl, an African. He is rather disdainful of her native culture, and calls her a barbarian:

> I must go back for more of her stilted talk, it's quite quaint, she is afraid she'll lose her language, I wondered why, or what it meant to her, she cannot read or write so why mourn a distant tongue ...

But there is an ironic interplay between her fear of losing her language and the fear, articulated by the real Ovid in his exile poetry, of forgetting Latin and only being able to speak the barbarian northern tongue of Tomis. (In fact for Ovid it is far more likely that the term barbarian would have been associated with northern types, such as Anglo-Saxons, than with people from Africa which, although exotic, lay within the Roman cultural pale.)

Gods

Although many classical texts – most famously Homer's *Iliad* and *Odyssey* – portray the gods of Olympus as faulty quasi-human characters, who love, hate, behave badly and make mistakes, Ovid takes this process a step further, frequently criticising or poking fun at his deities. This is Juno's reaction to hearing that her rival Callisto (whom she had turned into a bear as a punishment for her liaison with Jupiter) has been transformed into a star (2.520-6):

> Oh, what great things have I achieved! How vast is my power! I took away her human form – and now she has become a goddess! So this is how I punish my enemies – this is what

my great power amounts to! All it needs now is for him to free her from her animal form and give her back her old face as he did with Io. Now that I have been cast aside I don't know why he doesn't install her in the bedroom and become Lycaon's son-in-law.

Her sarcasm, spite and self-pity make her very human, if not in a particularly attractive way. The final dig, at the very unwelcome in-laws Callisto would bring into Olympus' first family, strikes a domestic and somehow modern note – indeed her surprisingly realistic and human snobbery allows us to make an unexpected connection with another spiteful, rejected female, Caroline Bingley in *Pride and Prejudice*. When her pretensions to Mr Darcy are threatened by Elizabeth Bennett, Miss Bingley lashes out by reminding Darcy how galling it would be to have the insufferable Mrs Bennett as a mother-in-law – 'You will have a charming mother-in-law, indeed, and of course she will be always at Pemberley with you.'

Ovid draws several comic parallels between the gods' existence and that of men, with the effect of making the former seem almost comically mundane. We generally imagine the gods operating on an elevated plane, but Ovid introduces little scraps of information which hint at a very human, almost humdrum, existence. We are given a glimpse of the gods' home life when Jupiter calls a council meeting to tell his subjects about the crime Lycaon has committed (1.170-6):

> The gods travel along the Milky Way to the halls and royal palace of the great Thunderer. On either side the doors of the high-ranking gods' dwellings are flung open, and their entrance halls swarm with visitors. (Lower-class gods live in a different quarter.) In this neighbourhood only the most cele-

Introduction

brated heaven dwellers have established their household gods. And this is the place, if I might be so bold, which I would scarcely hesitate to call the Palatia of Heaven.

There is an amusing and unexpected precision in Ovid's emphasis on the physical specificities of divine life. We may be aware of a hierarchy among gods, but we don't press this vague knowledge to its logical conclusion – that some parts of heaven are classier than others. (One might say Dante does this when he takes us through Heaven via ascending circles, but his account doesn't smack of house prices in the same way Ovid's does.) Further little details – such as a passing reference to Jupiter selecting his second-best lightning bolts in a vain effort to save the life of Semele after she has insisted on seeing him in full divine regalia – compound this effect. Another wooer, Mercury, primps himself amusingly before making contact with the beautiful Herse – he 'arranges his mantle so that it may hang becomingly, and makes sure that its golden border is clearly visible' (2.733-4).

The slightly jarring effect of this mixture of the banal and the elevated might be compared to that created by Terry Pratchett when he gives Death a horse named Binky or invents a fifth horseman of the apocalypse who left before the others became famous. Or indeed to the effect created by comparing a revered classical text with a comic fantasy novel. The Powell and Pressburger film *A Matter of Life and Death* (1946) is particularly Ovidian in its presentation of the afterlife. The angels conduct business rather in the manner of civil servants – the hero's guide is called 'angel 71' – and their hierarchy and bureaucracy are clearly defined. God seems to be keeping up with mankind's advances: new angels travel to heaven on a moving staircase and carefully carry their wings in dry cleaning bags. Heaven even has a Coke machine. If the Powell and Pressburger angels have learned from humanity's technological advances, so have Ovid's gods. Just before the assassination of Julius Caesar, Venus begs Jupiter to save him – he advises her to consult the gods' *rerum tabularia*, the 'public record office' to see for herself that Caesar's fate is sealed – an ultra-Roman detail which was probably inserted for comic effect, rather as though a modern poet were to depict God using Microsoft Excel to work out who gets into Heaven.

In fact the *Metamorphoses* is full of anachronisms that modern readers will tend to overlook because, for most of us, classical antiquity is a time-free zone. But Ovid's readers would have seen details such as the description of Diana and her attendants as amusingly modern and decidedly Roman – she is a typical *matrona* surrounded by her slave girls (3.167-72):

> Another attendant drapes the goddess' discarded robe over her arm. Two untie her shoelaces, while Theban Crocale, who is more accomplished than the others, gathers the goddess' rippling locks into a knot, while her own hair remains unbound. Nephele, Hyale, Rhanis, Psecas and Phiale fill brimming urns.

The effect achieved by mapping the customs and accoutrements of a sophisticated urban society onto an archaic mythical world is paralleled in the Disney film *Hercules*. The Greek world Hercules inhabits clearly mirrors the United States – Thebes is known as 'the Big Olive' and the superhero endorses his own brand of trainers and soft drinks. (If you find Disney films annoying the parallel works even better – Ovid's flip approach to his work seriously irritated many of his contemporaries.)

Introduction

If Ovid's gods were like powerful Romans, then Jupiter and Augustus might be thought to have a special bond, and this is certainly suggested when (in the passage quoted above) Ovid compares Jupiter's dwelling to the Roman imperial palace, or Palatia, and, later in the same episode, assures Augustus that Jupiter is just as pleased as he is when his subjects are loyal. But the link does not work quite as comfortably or flatteringly as we might expect. Augustus, with his obsession with family values, might not have wanted to be associated with the morally lax and intermittently rapacious Jupiter. Even episodes which seem to show the god in a more authoritative and judicial role have a disconcerting edge. The story of Lycaon is a telling example, for it is narrated by Jupiter himself. Augustus was an expert propagandist, and Jupiter similarly manipulates his rhetoric to ensure that all the lesser gods are 'on message'. A hint that Jupiter is in control of the narrative is given when Ovid reminds us that the story he is about to tell was 'still unpublished because the events were so recent' (1.164) – Jupiter will be responsible for how Lycaon is remembered.

Jupiter's rhetoric is impressive, and he carefully softens his audience up with portentous generalities before explaining the precise reason for his wrath (1.190-1):

Every solution must first be tried, but if the problem doesn't respond to treatment it must be cut away with a knife.

It turns out that when Jupiter visited the king in human form, Lycaon attempted to serve him with human flesh in order to test the god's divinity. By the time Jupiter gets round to telling heaven about this scandal, however, Lycaon has already spontaneously metamorphosed into a wolf. As everyone else Jupiter encountered worshipped him respectfully, it would seem that no

Ovid

action is really needed. But even though he has assured heaven that 'every solution must first be tried', Jupiter goes on to decree that the whole of humankind be destroyed in a flood, making way for a new and improved race of men to be created. As we shall see when we look at the stories of Actaeon and Arachne in more detail in later chapters, the justice of the gods' treatment of mortals is frequently very suspect.

Women

The presentation of women in the poem has been the subject of much recent discussion. Ovid's attitude towards them has been characterised as voyeuristic, even sadistic, but many have made a case for a proto-feminist Ovid who sympathises with his heroines and their difficulties. A jaundiced reader might wonder why, if Ovid likes women so much, he again and again depicts them as victims of rape, mutilation or punitive metamorphosis. A number of male writers have generated similar unease in their female readers – Thomas Hardy, for example, simultaneously appears to champion and punish his heroines, most famously the tragic Tess, who is hanged for murder after many misfortunes. We may view Hardy's apparent solicitous sympathy for Tess in a different light if we have also read his account of a hanging he witnessed aged just sixteen. Later, in his eighties, he recorded the impact this gruesome spectacle had upon him: 'what a fine figure she showed against the sky as she hung in the misty rain, and how the tight black silk gown set off her shape as she wheeled half round and back.'

But even though Ovid might fall similarly foul of the political correctness police, he is undeniably *interested* in women. One of his major poems, the *Heroides*, comprises a series of fictional letters written by mythical and historical women,

Introduction

including Dido and Helen, to their lovers; in giving these heroines – some of whom are comparatively marginal figures – a voice, he often makes us aware of the particular difficulties facing women, consciously offering a different perspective from that implicit in the male-dominated, usually epic works which form his sources. (In another parallel drawn from the Victorian novel we might compare Sue Roe's *Estella: Her Expectations* – an adaptation of Dickens' *Great Expectations* written from the point of view of its mysterious heroine.) Ovid's *Art of Love* similarly manifests an interest in the female perspective; although the first two books of this poem instruct young men how to get girls into bed, in the last book the tables are turned and Ovid advises girls how best to entice men. However, it shouldn't be assumed that Ovid's motives for this reversal were egalitarian, or indeed that women were the intended readers of Book 3.

Ovid's only tragedy, just two lines of which survive, focused on the troubled Medea, and his depiction of her in Book 7 of the *Metamorphoses* gives some indication of the effect this lost play might have produced. As a tortured, passionate woman, monstrous yet never quite alienating our sympathy, Medea is part of the tradition of striking 'anti-heroines' lying behind Lady Macbeth. Indeed Ovid's depiction of Medea's agonised thoughts as she hesitates, torn between love and duty, his evocation of the dynamic tension between opposing impulses, rather resembles a Shakespearean soliloquy (7.11-20):

> It is futile to resist – some god or other is standing in my way. I wouldn't be surprised if it were that thing called love – it is certainly something like it, for why do my father's orders seem so harsh to me? They certainly are too harsh. Why do I fear that Jason will die when I've only just clapped eyes upon him?

Why am I so afraid? Banish the flames of love from your virgin breast if you can, miserable Medea. I'd stop this madness if I could. But a strange force is pulling me even though I am unwilling. Desire draws me one way, reason another. I know full well which way is better but I follow the worse all the same.

Medea brings at least some of her troubles on her own head, but the *Metamorphoses* is full of women who suffer through no fault of their own. Io is first raped by Jupiter and then metamorphosed into a cow to conceal her from Juno's wrath. But Juno sees through the ruse, demands the heifer as a gift, and gives her to many-eyed Argus to guard (1.635-41):

When she imploringly tried to stretch out her arms towards Argus, she had no arms to stretch. She tried to complain, but could only moo. She started at the noise, and was terrified by her own voice. She arrived at the banks of her father Inachus' stream, where she had often played. But when she saw her gaping jaws and sprouting horns reflected in the stream, she was afraid, and fled, terrified of herself.

Io is eventually rescued by Mercury, who manages to send Argus to sleep by telling him the story of Syrinx – it remains unfinished because Argus falls asleep so quickly. There is a poignancy in the choice of Syrinx as the subject of this tale. She is yet another victim of male lust, chased by Pan until, rather like Daphne, she escapes through metamorphosis into reeds. From the reader's point of view there may be a joke here – we, by this time, are also perhaps a bit bored with rape narratives. But from Io's point of view Argus' boredom is a grim reminder that male violence against women is an everyday

Introduction

occurrence, not worth staying awake for. Chaucer creates a similar effect in the first fragment of *The Canterbury Tales* where he offers us a succession of comic tales of sexual intrigue. The inimitable Miller's Tale is followed by the rather less compelling Reeve's Tale. The Cook then begins what promises to be a still further diminished variation on the same theme, only for the tale to stop abruptly after just forty lines. Chaucer, like Ovid, flirts dangerously with the reader's capacity for boredom.

It isn't only obviously appealing doe-eyed victims whom we are encouraged to pity. Iphis – the name, like Hilary and Evelyn, could be used for a boy or a girl – was brought up as a boy to save her from being put to death by her father. Before her birth he had informed his wife that (9.676-9):

> Women's lives are harder, and fortune denies them strength. Therefore (and may it not fall out thus) if it should happen that you give birth to a girl – I am unwilling to say such a shocking thing – let her be destroyed.

A wedding is planned between young Iphis and her friend Ianthe. Although Iphis is in love with Ianthe she is filled with despair at the thought that the marriage can never be consummated. We are encouraged to feel sorry for Iphis, although Ovid also (I think) injects comedy into her complaint. She reflects miserably that 'cows don't love cows, nor mares, mares'. In fact cows often attempt to mate with other cows when on heat, and generally Iphis' sense of her own perversity seems rather exaggerated – she compares herself unfavourably with Pasiphaë, mother of the minotaur, who persuaded a bull to mate with her by disguising herself as a heifer. Iphis goes on to observe that 'if all the inventive skill in the world should be centred here, if Daedalus himself should fly back on his waxen wings, what could he contrive with his skill? (741-3). I think we may be supposed to snigger at this point – why does Ovid get her to invoke, not a god or enchanter, but an inventor of artefacts? – but the innocent Iphis is saved from her quandary by the intervention of the goddess Isis, who turns her into a boy at the altar.

A still more unlikely focus for our sympathy is Medusa. At the conclusion of the long and excitingly swashbuckling adventures of Perseus, when he and his cronies are relaxing over a meal, he is asked how he gained his secret weapon, the head of the gorgon Medusa which turns all who see it to stone. He briefly explains that he killed her when she was asleep, before going on to tell more tales of derring-do. Only when he is asked why Medusa had serpents for hair do we learn the gorgon's history (4.794-801):

> She used to be a celebrated beauty, and many suitors vied for her favour. Her hair was her best feature – I was told this by someone who claimed to have seen her. It is said that Neptune, ruler of the ocean, raped her in Minerva's temple. The daughter of Jupiter turned away in loathing and shielded her chaste countenance behind her aegis. And so the deed might not go unpunished, she changed the gorgon's locks into foul serpents.

This little narrative is all the more shocking because it is so coldly and casually told – Perseus seems to have no sense of the unfairness of her punishment, of the cruelty displayed by both Neptune and Minerva, and nor does he reflect on whether he was justified in killing her. Yet Ovid, I like to think, was acutely aware of all these factors.

Introduction

Men

But it would be very misleading to suggest that the *Metamorphoses* is full of wronged women and wicked men. The beautiful youth, Hermaphroditus, falls victim to a man-eating nymph, Salmacis, who assaults him while he bathes. Ovid's imagery nicely captures the counter-intuitive quality of female sexual aggression. The snake at first seems to be the victim in her encounter with the eagle, ivy is (ostensibly) far more fragile than an oak tree, and the polyp attacks by enclosing rather than penetrating (4.361-7):

> And then, though he struggles to escape, she entwines herself round him, like a serpent whom an eagle has seized and borne away on high; thus dangling, the snake clasps his head and feet, and binds his beating wings with her tail. Salmacis also resembles the ivy, which often weaves itself around great tree trunks, and the squid, which immobilises its captive prey under water with its tentacles.

It is difficult to avoid a touch of absurdity, if not downright comedy, when depicting the victims of predatory females. But when the predator is a goddess the danger is more acute, and is treated with corresponding seriousness. Although she cannot, like her male counterparts, force handsome Picus to become her lover, Circe is able to punish him severely for his disdain. 'You will find out what a woman crossed in love can do – and Circe is a woman crossed in love' (14.384-5) she cries, and turns him into a woodpecker. When his companions venture to protest at this harsh treatment she unhesitatingly changes all of them into beasts too.

Men who err the other way, and force their attentions on goddesses, are liable to receive similar punishments. We may not particularly sympathise with the violent Pyreneus, who falls to his death attempting to chase the winged muses off a tower, but Actaeon, who only happens to come across the naked Diana, and is turned into a stag and killed by his own hounds, is surely to be pitied.

Ovid is very good at debunking typically 'masculine' pretensions of various kinds. When he beholds the chained princess Andromeda about to be attacked by a sea monster, Perseus addresses the weeping girl and her grieving parents in the following pompous speech (4.695-702):

> You will soon have plenty of time for weeping, but there is little time left for helping. If I sought this girl as the son of Jupiter and of Danaë, whom Jupiter filled with fecund gold when she was imprisoned, or as Perseus, victor of the snaky locked gorgon, who dared to fly though the air on fluttering wings, I would certainly be your first choice as a son-in-law. And now, if the gods will permit, I shall try to add the merit of being really useful to all my other gifts.

When reading the story quickly it is easy to miss the jokes here because we just assume that successful heroes are heroic. But in fact Perseus betrays his weaknesses in various ways, We have already been told by Ovid that Perseus is a timid flyer – he is nervous about flying at night – and we will soon learn that his great victory over Medusa consisted of killing her when she was asleep. And why, if 'there is little time left for helping', is he boasting of his manly prowess rather than getting on with the rescue? Sara Mack describes the comic bathos of Perseus' final triumph. 'When the going gets rough [he] simply takes out his trusty Gorgon's head and petrifies the last two hundred of the enemy' (126). Superior technology is used to create a similar

Introduction

sort of comic anticlimax in *Raiders of the Lost Ark* when Indiana Jones, faced by a dazzling display of scimitarsmanship from his opponent as he warms up for a fight, simply pulls out his gun and shoots him.

Brawny Hercules is also the butt of Ovid's humour. When he and his bride Deianira are faced with a swollen, turbulent river, Hercules takes at face value the centaur Nessus' offer to carry Deianira over safely while Hercules makes his own way across. As well as being foolishly trusting, Hercules indulges in pointless heroics: 'He neither hesitated nor made any effort to find the least turbulent spot – indeed he scorned to take advantage of the smoother water' (9.116-17). Hercules wins back Deianira fairly easily, but in the next book we are introduced to a husband who braves far more for the sake of his wife. Orpheus' bride Eurydice dies soon after their marriage when she is bitten on the ankle by a snake. Famously, Orpheus goes down to the Underworld to beg for her return. But in Ovid's version little is done to make the poet's feat seem in any way exceptional – no barriers are put in his way, and the whole trip seems no more daunting than going through the Channel Tunnel. Even when he delivers his speech to Pluto and Proserpina we aren't really given the impression of a grieving widower. He injects a little facetious urbanity into his plea when he cites (in a rather knowing, coy way) Proserpina's abduction as proof that love is common to all (10.26-9):

> But I have been conquered by Love, a god who is celebrated on earth, though I'm not sure whether that is the case down below – yet I suspect that he is just as well known here, for unless the old story of that abduction is false, Love joined you two together as well.

Ovid

Because Orpheus seems such an oddly cool customer, the description of how even the 'bloodless shades' were moved to tears by his plea seems rather unconvincing. Once Orpheus has lost Eurydice for a second and final time (when he looks back at her before they have left the Underworld) a further jarring, bathetic note is introduced. We are told that he rejected the love of women, even though many loved him. Such behaviour seems touchingly loyal – but when Ovid goes on to inform us that Orpheus transferred his affections to young boys the effect, if not comic precisely, is far from tragic.

Structure

Ovid seems to play with his poem's resistance to structure and order in various ways. One obvious example is his placement of book divisions. Many of the poem's fifteen books end in the middle of stories rather than at one of the many 'natural' breaks between tales. A teasing example is that between Books 2 and 3. Book 2 ends with the abduction of Europa by Jupiter in the form of a bull. But Book 3 brushes the story's ending aside in a single sentence, with no reference to any sexual liaison between Europa and her abductor – 'Now the god, having put aside his disguise and owned his true identity, reached the fields of Crete' (3.1-2). It may be that Ovid signals his own awareness of the way he is breaking the story at an exciting point when, at the very end of Book 2, he describes Europa clutching one of the bull's horns as she is carried away from the shore. To a modern reader this detail perhaps seems sexually suggestive, but it might have had a further resonance within a Roman context. The principal meaning of *cornu* was an animal's horn, but the same word was also used to describe the end of a stick around which books were rolled. 'So might

Introduction

the reader be holding on to the horn of the book and wondering, like Europa, what next?' (Wheeler 93). This odd link between the poem's events and its physical existence as a bookroll is reprised in the way Book 8 segues into Book 9. Book 8 ends with the river-god Acheloüs explaining that he has lost one of his horns and groaning with misery. Book 9 begins, as though there has been no pause, with Theseus asking him to explain the reason for his mutilated forehead. The Latin word *frons* means forehead, but was also used to signify the outer end of a book roll. Thus the phrase 'truncae (mangled, truncated) ... frontis' might refer to the deformed forehead of Acheloüs or, more obliquely, to the way the narrative has been chopped in half by the arbitrary book division.

The links between stories are still more noteworthy. At the very beginning of the poem the narrator promises his readers a 'perpetual song' and, even though he has so very many stories to tell, Ovid weaves them together in an endless variety of ways, and makes particularly inventive use of multiple narrators – the tale of Atalanta is told by Venus to Adonis, while their story is itself told by a still further inset narrator, Orpheus. More often than not, unless we're consciously looking out for them, we don't even notice the way tales are linked together, but are swept along by the poem's buoyant momentum. But sometimes we feel Ovid is encouraging us to notice the occasional moment of comically shaky continuity. On more than one occasion he uses a person's absence or non-involvement in events as an excuse to embark on their story. For example, after the funeral of Aesacus, because Ovid wants to begin his Trojan War narrative, we are told that 'Paris was not present on this sad occasion, Paris, who would soon bring prolonged war to his homeland with his stolen wife' (12.4-6). Another clever join between two unconnected tales is forged later in the same book (12.536-40):

As Nestor related the conflict between the Lapiths and the Centaurs, Tlepolemus couldn't keep quiet when Hercules was passed over without a mention, and said: 'I am amazed that you have forgotten to praise the deeds of Hercules ...'.

As well as playing around with the idea of story-telling, manipulating or cheating the reader's expectations of narrative drive, Ovid disrupts our sense of the integrity of his imagined world. Its chronology, in particular, doesn't quite compute. For example Callisto's father, as I've already briefly mentioned, was Lycaon. Her story is told after that of Lycaon, and clearly the enmity between him and Jupiter is established, for, as we have already seen, Juno refers to it when she taunts Jupiter. Yet Lycaon's unnatural behaviour caused Jupiter to flood the earth, leaving only Pyrrha, Deucalion and the new race created from stones to survive. How can Lycaon's daughter have slipped through the net? It has been suggested that the placement of this story is significant – Jupiter glimpses Callisto while (in another amusingly literal-minded evocation of divinity) checking that Phaëthon's exploits with the chariot of the sun haven't caused too much damage: 'But now the Almighty Father makes a survey of heaven's high walls and checks to see whether anything has been weakened or loosened as a result of the raging fire' (2.401-3). Is it possible, as Andrew Zissos and Ingo Gildenhard suggest, that Phaëthon's mismanagement of the sun (as the sun is so bound up with our sense of time) has created some kind of temporal distortion, a disruption in the space-time continuum allowing Callisto to spring into existence? If we reject this science-fictional response to the apparent glitch it is still possible that Ovid wasn't simply being forgetful. He likes to keep his readers on their toes and often disconcerts us by

Introduction

hinting at his own unreliability. As well as casting doubt on poets' tales in Pythagoras' speech, he encourages the reader's scepticism at various other points, as when he introduces Scylla: 'She had the face of a virgin, and if poets' tales are not all lies, was once a virgin indeed' (13.733-4). Yet scepticism is a dangerous quality in the poem – Pentheus is torn apart in punishment for doubting the divinity of Bacchus and, less dramatically, Theseus' friend Pirithoüs elicits a reaction of shock and disapproval from his companions when he speaks sneeringly of metamorphic myths (8.614-15):

> 'These are just stories, Achelous,' he said, 'and you impute too much power to the gods when you claim that they can change people's shape'.

In order to convince the sceptic that he is mistaken, Lelex tells the story of Baucis and Philemon. Homely details – when Jupiter and Mercury come to dine Baucis has to stabilise the table with a potsherd because its legs are different lengths – certainly create an air of verisimilitude, and Lelex supplies arresting testimony to the reality of the old couple's final metamorphosis into trees (8.719-22):

> And to this day the Bithynian peasant points out the neighbouring trees, growing from a double trunk. I was told this by serious old men who had no reason to lie.

But when a rather similar rhetoric of proof and certainty is used by one of Ovid's many internal narrators, Vertumnus, we may, retrospectively, wonder just how convincing Lelex's arguments are. Vertumnus tells the nymph Pomona the tale of heartless Anaxarete who turned to stone after her suitor (another Iphis) committed suicide. Because he wants to persuade Pomona to sleep with him, and shun the example of hard-hearted Anaxarete, Vertumnus adds this portentous assurance of the tale's veracity: 'And so that you won't think this just a story, there is still a statue in the princess' image in Salamis to this day', before adding rather inconsequentially 'Salamis also contains a temple in honour of the Gazing Venus' (14.758-61). Unlike Lelex's old men, Iphis *does* have a reason to deceive, and we might well reflect that although the reality of any particular tree or statue may be proved, further evidence is needed to demonstrate that these things are the result of metamorphosis.

This possible potential bond between the stories told by Vertumnus and Lelex is just one little example of the hundreds of parallels and connections the reader may spot in the *Metamorphoses*. So many nuances are lost when one reads the stories anthologised out of order or in isolation. A grisly example comes in Ovid's account of Pentheus, who doubted the divinity of Bacchus and received a horrible punishment. A repeated motif in the *Metamorphoses*, which the attentive reader would have picked up on by this stage (the end of Book 3), is the poignant post-metamorphic moment when the victim attempts to stretch his arms out beseechingly to a friend or relative but cannot because he no longer has arms. Typical is Io: 'When she imploringly tried to stretch out her arms towards Argus, she had no arms to stretch' (1.635-6). Pentheus' situation taps into this motif but his lack of arms has a more grotesque cause than metamorphosis. His mother and aunts are maddened by Bacchic frenzy (3.721-6):

> She tears off the pleader's right arm. The frenzied Ino tears off the other. The miserable man has no arms to stretch out

Introduction

to his mother, but shows her his mutilated stumps, the limbs torn away, and cries 'O mother, look at me'. Agave ... rips his head off.

And if the reader still remembers this grisly tale by the time Book 6 is reached another link may be made. Sisters Procne and Philomela (discussed in Chapter 3) tear apart Procne's young son Itys following a similar Bacchanal. The two stories are in many ways quite dissimilar, but in both we find sisters, Bacchic frenzy, a son murdered by his mother and the subsequent *sparagmos* – or ritual tearing apart of a hero.

But there is no real limit to the amount and variety of links which can be formed between the poem's many tales. The tale of Philomela may take us back to Pentheus, but is equally likely to make us reflect on Philomela's affinities with her fellow-weaver, Arachne, or with Scylla and her father Nisus, who also shockingly transgress their ties of kinship, and are similarly turned into birds to avoid bloodshed. It is common to talk of the *Metamorphoses* as a woven poem because the tales are so tightly enmeshed together; however, as the nodes between them are almost inexhaustible and are not constrained by their location in the poem, it is really more like a miniature world wide web than a tapestry.

Of course this analogy only works up to a point – it would be doing a disservice to Ovid's art to suggest that there is no significance in the ordering of his tales. Sometimes a clue to our intended response may be hidden if we read a tale out of context. The goddess Latona seems a victim to be pitied when a 'rustic rabble' prevents her drinking from their pool. We are particularly inclined to sympathise with Latona when she begs the peasants to take pity on her twin babies (6.358-60):

Ovid

'And let these children, who stretch out their little arms from my breast, move your pity.' And by chance the children did stretch out their arms. Who would not have been moved by the goddess' gentle words?

The rhetorical question gains an ironic edge, however, if we remember that we have just been reading about these same children's adult exploits. When Niobe boasted that she had more children than Latona, the goddess told the twins, Diana and Apollo, to punish her. Resisting all pleas for mercy, they shot dead Niobe's seven daughters and seven sons. As we hear of Latona's own plea for mercy less than 100 lines later, the pathos of the babies' plight may ring hollow. We might even wonder whether the babies really stretch out their arms 'by chance', or whether, rather like John Wyndham's 'Midwich Cuckoos', they are responding to their mother's cue with sinister precocity. Certainly the very next story should persuade the reader of the family's cruelty, for we are told in agonising detail of the fate of Marsyas, flayed alive for challenging Apollo to a music contest and losing. (The deal was that the winner was allowed to do whatever he wanted to the loser.) (6.387-91):

> The skin is stripped off his limbs as he screams, and his whole body is one massive wound. Blood streams down his sides, his sinews lie revealed; his trembling veins quiver with no skin to cover them. You could count his beating organs, and the entrails were clearly visible in his breast.

The background to this horrible act is summarised in a single sentence – 'another remembered the satyr who had been beaten by the son of Latona in a piping contest, and punished' (6.383-5) – allowing us to meditate with horrified sympathy on his

Introduction

shocking end, memorably depicted in a late painting by Titian. In a typical example of the Ovidian wit so many readers have found reprehensible, Marsyas cries out to Apollo 'why do you tear me from myself?' Apollo's icy unconcern for the feelings of others is apparent from his debut in Book 1 of the *Metamorphoses*, in the first of many tales of unrequited lust, the account of his passion for the nymph Daphne.

1

Daphne

> She'll tell
> her story
> rather than be held inside its web. There are holes –
> have you noticed –
> where the seams don't quite close? Daphne peers through
> those gaps.
> She scans the sky and plans to stare – you can almost hear her
> glance –
> down the air, the blank, the optical until
> a face stares back
> Alice Fulton, 'Turn: a version'

The earth is quick to generate new life after the flood, summoned by Jupiter to punish mankind, subsides. Among the creatures brought forth is the monstrous Python, who terrifies the new race of men but is finally destroyed by Apollo's arrows. The god's pride in his victory prompts him to taunt Cupid, sneering that a mere boy has no business with a bow and arrow. Angered by Apollo's scorn, Cupid shoots him with a golden arrow which enflames him with love for Daphne, the virgin daughter of Peneus the river-god. Cupid then shoots Daphne with a leaden arrow to ensure she responds to the god's suit with horror. As Apollo pursues the fleeing nymph she begs her father to help her escape, and is transformed into a laurel. Apollo claims the tree as his own, to be a symbol of military and artistic triumph.

Ovid

This is one of the *Metamorphoses*' best known stories. Daphne's transformation has been depicted by numerous painters as well as by Bernini in his celebrated sculpture, and has also inspired composers, most famously Handel and Richard Strauss. One of the most striking recent literary adaptations of the myth, Alice Fulton's 'Daphne and Apollo', a quirky series of poems very loosely based on the *Metamorphoses*, was included in Michael Hofmann and James Lasdun's *After Ovid*. Her retelling is firmly embedded within its own cultural context, very different from that in which Ovid's own poem is enmeshed. In the third poem, 'Take: A Roman Wedding', Fulton reanimates the historical realities of Roman women's lives from a twentieth-century perspective, evoking the fear and helplessness of a girl forced into the kind of marriage Daphne is so anxious to avoid:

> Once upon a bride there was a time.
> Between twelve and twenty. But a minor
>
> all her life. Once – no often, every war –
> She was taken by force, as spoils, as lifting
> her over
>
> the threshold remembers.

Just as Fulton can read the unarticulated female point of view out of (or into) the literature of Roman men, so can she excavate a Daphne from the *Metamorphoses* whom Ovid probably wouldn't recognise:

> She could snuff a burning candle with a bullet,
> break
> five eggs before they hit the ground and pierce the ace of hearts.
> All with her back to the target, while aiming in her compact.

1. Daphne

In 'Turn: a version', quoted at the beginning of this chapter, Fulton seems to reflect on the problems inherent in this kind of modernisation. To what extent is a story able to freewheel, to generate new meanings and break free of its author's intentions and its historical context? Fulton seems to be suggesting that Daphne is like a fly trapped in a story web from which she must struggle to escape. Yet at the same time she appears to acknowledge that the story is not so constricting after all, that in fact it has a very open weave and can accommodate different readings. Fulton's feminist take on Daphne is perhaps already present, or potential at least, in Ovid's version. Certainly the afterlife of Ovid's brief narrative is astonishingly complex, and can, as Fulton implies, be seen as a battle fought over Daphne, as her story is reprised, reinvented, even completely reversed by countless writers who view her with pity, hostility, approval, irritation and laughter. This chapter charts Daphne as a contested site of interpretation from Ovid's own poem to some of the most recent responses to the myth.

The sharp divisions in the tale's reception may partly be explained by the tone of the original. The experiences of Apollo and Daphne, the amorous pursuer and the terrified victim, are clearly polarised in Ovid's narrative. We are encouraged to understand both points of view – that of Daphne is not privileged. Although himself in a sense a 'victim' – of Cupid's golden arrow which has kindled his desire for Daphne – Apollo seems less a thrall to love or even lust than an elegant connoisseur of the pleasures of the chase (1.504-11):

> Nymph, Peneus' daughter, – stay, I beg you. It is not a foe who chases you. Please stay! Thus the lamb flies from the wolf and the deer from the lion, thus doves fly from the eagle on fluttering wings, thus do all creatures flee from their enemies. But Love is the reason for my pursuit – woe is me! I am worried

that you will slip, and that thorns will tear your tender limbs –
I don't wish to cause you pain. The terrain over which you run
is rough. I beg you to run more slowly, and I will moderate my
own pace to match yours.

Although Apollo seeks to disassociate his own amorous pursuit
from that of a predator hunting its prey, the effect is to align the
nymph with such terrified victims, particularly in a poem which
so frequently compares victims of rape to hunted animals. And
Apollo's promise that if she will only slow down he will conscientiously moderate his own pace to match is cruelly unconvincing
in its wit. It is perhaps disturbing to modern readers that this cool
Apollonian wit seems so similar to the poet's own, and when Ovid
explains dispassionately that Daphne's wish for perpetual virginity
is incompatible with her appearance we may feel that the narrative is taking Apollo's side (1.488-9):

> Her father gave in to Daphne's request to remain a virgin. But
> your loveliness forbids the fulfilment of your desires, Daphne,
> and your beauty repulses your prayers.

By semi-personifying her beauty as an agent at war with her
wishes, Ovid seems almost to hint at her own complicity with
Apollo's pursuit. As there is no concrete evidence for this in the
action, as distinct from Ovid's own narrative gloss on events, it
might be fair to say that Ovid seems an unfairly Apollonian
narrator, who suspects that Daphne is just a little less reluctant
than she makes out.

Literary rapes (and attempted rapes) are frequently thus problematic. Victims – such as Mozart's Donna Anna, Samuel
Richardson's Clarissa and Amy, the female lead in Sam Peckinpah's
Straw Dogs – are tainted, or perceived to be tainted, by a sugges-

1. Daphne

tion of responsibility or secret pleasure. An extended and disturbingly equivocal account of rape is given in Shakespeare's *Rape of Lucrece*. Like Ovid, Shakespeare's narrator describes a heroine at war with herself; beauty's red and virtue's white compete for the face of Lucrece (68-70).

> Yet their ambition makes them still to fight,
> The sovereignty of either being so great
> That oft they interchange each other's seat.

Tarquin, the rapist, himself goes on to use a similar image of Lucrece at war with herself; her beauty, like that of Daphne, takes arms on behalf of the male aggressor. The affinity between the rapist's rhetoric and that of his narrator (similar to that in the *Metamorphoses*) hints that the telling is biased in some way (477-80):

> 'The colour in thy face,
> That even for anger makes the lily pale
> And the red rose blush at her disgrace,
> Shall plead for me and tell my loving tale'.

Returning to Daphne's plight, we seem to be further drawn in to an Apollonian perspective by the way we see, and in a sense participate in, his lingering gaze as it travels tantalisingly over her body, striptease style. As Daphne runs, the god's visual enjoyment is further enhanced when the wind blows away her hair and clothes, revealing still more of her body (1.527-30):

> The wind exposed her body to view, while opposing breezes ruffled her garments and made her locks stream out behind her. In flight she seemed still lovelier than before.

Ovid

The reader who knows Ovid's earlier *Art of Love* might well suspect that Daphne was partly complicit in the pursuit, for that poem's narrator counselled women to affect indifference in order to heighten their desirability and assured his male readers that women often secretly wish to be taken by force (1.665-6):

> She may struggle at first and cry 'you monster', yet she will hope to be overwhelmed in the struggle.

There are other hints in the text which encourage us to see Apollo and Ovid sharing similar goals. As a tree Daphne will serve Apollo's ends – she will flatter his art, adorning his hair, lyre and quiver. Daphne is similarly subservient to Ovid's artistic ambitions, and the narrator playfully alludes to this function through wordplay. We have already seen that Ovid likes to permeate the boundaries between the real world, in which the reader handles the text as a physical volume, and the fictive world of the poem. After her metamorphosis Daphne is enclosed in bark – *liber* – and her hair changes to foliage – *frons*. In Latin *liber* may mean book as well as bark, and, as we saw in the previous chapter, one meaning of *frons* is the outside of a book roll. Daphne is imprisoned not just within the laurel but within the pages of the *Metamorphoses* as well. Although neither Ovid nor Apollo enjoys Daphne sexually, they could be said to collaborate in an artistic exploitation of her transformed body.

But if she is a text she is an ambiguous text, one whose meanings are not confined to those which the narrator seems to intend. Just as Shakespeare's Tarquinian narrator should not be assumed to speak with Shakespeare's voice, so Ovid's narrator allows us plenty of room for interpretative manoeuvre – as indeed he also does in the *Art of Love*. The reader is not obliged to see events from a masculine, Apollonian, perspective. We are

1. Daphne

invited, for example, to interrogate Daphne's apparent final approval of her new role as Apollo's tree (1.566-7):

When Apollo had finished, the laurel inclined her branches and seemed to nod her leafy top.

The word 'seemed' is significant. The tree may be non-sentient, its top moved only by the wind. Or the movement may express a rejection of Apollo's plan; the verb used by Ovid to express the tree's movement – *agito* – to move or shake – could, like the English agitate, have connotations of disturbance or vexation. Presumably by chance, the Disney film *Hercules* includes a comic detail which might be interpreted as confirmation of a reluctant Daphne. The lecherous Philoctetes chases a bevy of nymphs only to watch in dismay as they all metamorphose into trees. Refusing to accept the evidence of his eyes, he assures Hercules that the nymphs can't keep their hands off him, only to have his statement confirmed when a nymph/tree slaps his face with her hand/branch. In Ovid the wooer's misreading of events is only one possibility, in the Disney film there is no such ambiguity, yet both play with the potential of language to tell different stories.

The narrative subtlety and complexity of Ovid's narrative, and the way both points of view are represented, encouraged later writers to approach the tale in sharply contrasting ways. Whereas earlier poets and commentators often reinvented Daphne as a variously faulty character, the twentieth century saw a number of writers, particularly women, rewriting the myth from an avowedly feminist perspective. Some of the most startling takes on Apollo and Daphne can be found in Christian commentaries on the poem. Such interpretations were frequently counter-intuitive and what might be described as a kind of institutionalised misogyny often recast women as villains, quite against the grain of the original text. Eurydice, for example, is figured by one such commentary as 'lust' whereas in Ovid's account she is a hapless and chaste victim, first of death, then of Orpheus' lack of self-restraint. Daphne is treated still more unfairly by some commentators; Pierre Bersuire, for example, writing in the fourteenth century, casts her as the reluctant synagogue, obstinately resisting the opportunity to convert to Christianity, while the would-be rapist Apollo is figured as Christ. Yet the commentary tradition is rich and varied, though very alien from modern sensibilities, and is by no means consistently anti-female in its bias. The fourteenth-century *Ovide moralisé* associated Daphne with the Virgin Mary, and John of Garland, writing in the thirteenth century, interpreted the myth as man's pursuit of wisdom. (Though interestingly this positive gloss on the nymph's role implies the desirability of Daphne's capture.)

The misogyny apparently inherent in medieval culture also affects even ostensibly neutral responses to Ovid's tale. Illustrations of the *Ovide moralisé* depict Daphne in the final stage of metamorphosis; her body has been turned into a tree but her human head remains visible, peeping out from the branches. Although the artist does not actively suggest that she is anything but a victim, the iconography of Western culture works against her, for images of Adam and Eve's temptation from the same period frequently depict a serpent with a woman's face entwined round the tree in the garden of Eden. Thus the misogynist impulse which gave Satan a sex change in medieval iconography might be said to have indirectly tainted representations of Daphne.

If we move forward five centuries or so we can find Satan and Daphne brought once again into curious complicity in a

1. Daphne

recent poem by William Wadsworth, 'The Snake in the Garden Considers Daphne'. Satan addresses the transformed nymph:

> up there it seems to be all light
> and prelapsarian elation – but bear
> in mind your lower half that gropes
> for water, the slender roots you spread
> in secret to fascinate the rocks,
> while sunlight pries apart your leaves
> and flights of birds arouse the air
> around you.

Here Satan seems to imply that Daphne is less pure, more consciously alluring, than she pretends to be, and at the end of the poem he binds her closer to him, morally, when he casts them both as comparable figures of temptation, even though Daphne is an unwitting and unwilling 'temptress' while Satan sets out deliberately to entrap and destroy:

> We cannot grasp
> The word hope, which the ones we've tempted
> Find always at their fingertips

Although the association of Daphne with Satan is rather an unusual and extreme example of a misogynistic response to her story, the nymph is repeatedly viewed in a cynical light. In particular, it is frequently assumed (or at least pretended) that Daphne did not deserve her reputation for chastity. And if her virginity is allowed, its merit is compromised in various ways. Even in a broadly accurate, though burlesque, seventeenth-century retelling of the tale, Thomas Brown refers to her fleeing

Ovid

Apollo 'like a whore from a constable freed'. Although the action of his poem mirrors that of Ovid's tale, the terms of this particular comparison, like some of the hostile medieval interpretations, cast her as the transgressor and Apollo as the upholder of order. Another poet at work in the same period, Henry Bold, suggests that Daphne's refusal was a matter of taste rather than principle when, in a poem addressed to Charles II, he assures the king that:

> Had Phoebus ever shone so fair as this
> Daphne had scaped her metamorphosis

Whereas Bold doesn't question the mythical chastity of Daphne, merely hypothesises her inability to withstand Charles, other writers contorted the legend, recasting the virtuous nymph as an adulteress. Here is a Victorian variation on the joke, penned by Horace Smith (the 'memento' is not the original laurel wreath but the horns traditionally ascribed to cuckolds):

> Daphne, like many another fair,
> To whom connubial ties are horrid,
> Fled from his arms, but left a rare
> Memento sprouting on his forehead.

By sleight of hand Smith maps a straying wife's aversion to one particular, established 'connubial tie' – she flees from her husband because she craves variety – onto virginal Daphne's quite different aversion to marriage as an institution.

Indeed male writers' capacity to find ways of casting Daphne's behaviour in the worst possible light seems almost unbounded. Jonathan Swift offers a sneering explanation for her disinclination:

1. Daphne

> For such is all the sex's flight
> They fly from learning, wit and light.
> They fly, and none can overtake
> But some gay coxcomb or a rake.

Swift, like the author of the *Ovide moralisé*, does not deny Daphne's genuine reluctance but puts an unfavourable gloss on it nonetheless. Like Smith, he has refigured Daphne's terrified flight from rape as mere flightiness. A number of other poets recast her reluctance as unjustified, implying that a woman should not thwart a man's desires however unwilling she might be. In an early seventeenth-century poem by Richard Barnfield, for example, Apollo tells Cassandra that Daphne's metamorphosis was a punishment:

> Who for she would not to my will agree,
> The gods transformed into a laurell tree.

However (as he is trying to persuade Cassandra to be less cold than Daphne) it may be Apollo who is deliberately misinterpreting the story rather than the poet getting it wrong. Earlier the Elizabethan poet Edmund Spenser put a similar spin on the legend in one of his *Amoretti*; here too it is implied that the narrator is mistelling the story for his own amorous ends as he addresses his beloved:

> Proud Daphne scorning Phoebus' lovely fire
> On the Thessalian shore from him did flee:
> For which the gods in their revengeful ire
> Did her transform into a laurel tree.

Although in these two examples Daphne is described as in some way to blame, the context ensures that the effect is more playful than misogynistic. The speaker is (more or less securely) differentiated from the poet, and we are implicitly allowed, even invited, to resist his line of argument.

Alice Fulton crystallises and exaggerates Apollo's misogyny in order to increase our sympathy for Daphne. His response to her metamorphosis, for example, appears bizarrely perverse:

> Of course, he liked her better as a tree. 'Girls *are* trees'
> was his belief. Mediated
> forms pleased him. 'If you can't find a partner, use
> a wooden chair' ...

But this curious preference is anticipated in several much earlier responses to the myth. A strange, vegetal sexuality, silent and acquiescent, is oddly hinted at in several medieval illustrations of Daphne. These invert Ovid's implied metamorphic sequence – the transformation of her head is described at the very end of his account – depicting her with a leafy top and a woman's body. The narrator of Andrew Marvell's 'The Garden' unambiguously suggests a preference for trees over women:

> When we have run our passions heat,
> Love hither makes his best retreat.
> The gods that mortal beauty chase,
> Still in a tree did end their race.
> Apollo hunted Daphne so,
> Only that she might laurel grow.
> And Pan did after Syrinx speed,
> Not as a nymph but for a reed.

The narrator's love of trees might seem innocuous, the garden itself a bucolic and anti-erotic idyll. But this isn't the whole story. He describes foliage in almost sexual terms, as a direct

1. Daphne

replacement for women – an alternative object of desire, not a means of escaping desire:

> No white nor red was ever seen
> So am'rous as this lovely green.
>
> The luscious clusters of the vine
> Upon my mouth do crush their wine;
> The nectarene and curious peach,
> Into my hands themselves do reach ...

We might wonder whether the 'race' which the gods end in a tree connotes not a running contest but a species, doomed by strange miscegeny to extinction. A similar grotesque possibility is suggested in 'Noon Vision', written by the early twentieth-century poet Thomas Sturge Moore; this is his description of the god's acceptance of Daphne's change:

> And must a god then feel dismay,
> Seeking a mouth, to find a flower?
> Or ...! an effect of divine power,
> Was this thy will? ...
> This blossom, this fair open thing
> That holds no secret from the world?
> Not like a mouth

All these poets are of course male. Women poets often swerved the other way, making the legend more, not less, woman-friendly. Daphne, as the laurel, is primarily associated with poetry, and is thus frequently invoked when praise is given to poets. Daphne's transformation into a laurel seems to cast the woman in an acquiescent, purely supportive role by contrast with the creative male poet of genius. But her function subtly changes when the poet being praised is female. In a flattering poem addressed to the Restoration poet Aphra Behn for example:

> The female laurels were obscured till now,
> And they deserved the shades in which they grew.
> But Daphne at your call returns her flight,
> Looks boldly up, and dares the god of light.

Daphne is no longer a passive commodity, gift of a god to future male poets, but the active ally of a female poet who wishes to outdo her male predecessors – a little later in the poem Aphra Behn is assured that 'If love's the theme, you outdo Ovid's art'. The victory of Behn over Ovid mirrors Daphne's triumph over Apollo. It is possible that more is being said here than that Behn was an unusually gifted female poet. By suggesting a reversal of the Daphne legend, the nymph is empowered but also subtly sexualised. She is after all fleeing a rape rather than any other kind of attack, so her decision to face rather than avoid the challenge implies a willingness to co-operate with the god's desires rather than valour – the word 'boldly' (when used of a woman's glance) commonly suggested sexual immodesty. Behn has perhaps mastered Ovid in the practice as well as in the theory of love's arts.

Daphne is invoked as proof of female poetic superiority even more strongly, and less equivocally, in a poem addressed to another seventeenth-century poet, Katherine Philips, by 'Philo-Philippa':

> Thee I invoke Orinda, for my Muse;
> He could but force a branch, Daphne her tree
> Most freely offers to her sex and thee,

1. Daphne

> And says to verse so unconstrained as yours,
> Her laurel freely comes, your fame secures;
> And men no longer shall with ravished bays
> Crown their forced poems by as forced a praise.

And Charles Goodall, in a poem about a lesser known contemporary of Behn's, Mrs Wright, simply says: 'Daphne to laurel turned, a female brow/ Has the best title to a female bough'.

A particularly interesting twist on this co-option of Daphne by, or on behalf of, women poets is offered by the eighteenth-century bluestocking, Elizabeth Carter, in a poem written to a young lady who aspires to be a poet. Whereas the connection forged by Philo-Philippa between the pursuit of 'laurels' and the pursuit of Daphne as a sexual object was merely epigrammatic and opportunistic, Carter emphasises the link, invoking literary success as a kind of *jouissance*:

> Let not ungentle Daphne's scorn
> Thy rising hopes restrain
> Apollo, pow'r of wit and verse,
> Her favour sued in vain.

The young poetess is assured that:

> Repeated efforts shall prevail
> And gain the beauteous prize.

Apollo is indeed the god of wit and poetry, but his pursuit of the nymph was sexual, not literary. The slippage between Daphne as erotic object and crown of poetic ambition is of course more striking because the wooer, the poem's addressee, is a woman. (If she were a man one might suspect a play on the word 'rising'.)

Ovid

The need to recast the traditional pattern of male poet and female muse, and the acknowledgement that any disruption of this pattern may constitute a sexual as well as a literary transgression, is implicit in a poem by the American Modernist poet, Hilda Doolittle ('HD'), 'If you will let me sing'. Here she seems to address a male poet or the male literary establishment, restoring a gender balance to inspiration by aligning Daphne with Hyacinthus, another (male) love of Apollo's. The function of Muse or inspiration seems to have shifted back to Apollo, with Daphne and Hyacinthus acting as intermediaries who will ensure that both men and women can gain access to the god.

> If you will let me sing,
> That God will be
> gracious to each of us,
> who found his own wild Daphne
> in a tree,
> who set
> on desolate plinth,
> image
> of Hyacinth.

Although HD's seems a plea for simple equality, implicit in many of the earlier poems in praise of poetesses is the notion of a battle between the sexes, and a certain pleasure in the god's discomfiture. But just as not all male poets skewed the myth in Daphne's disfavour (many of the flattering verses quoted above are by men), not all women poets have simply championed Daphne as a totem of female virtue or female genius. Her virtue, in particular, has not been found universally appealing. We have already seen how Daphne was used ostensibly to flatter Aphra

1. Daphne

Behn, but possibly also to hint at her sexual experience. Behn's poetry is certainly not coy. One of her best known erotic poems is 'The Disappointment'. Its heroine, Chloris, flees her lover Lysander as Daphne fled Apollo:

> Like lightning through the grove she hies,
> Or Daphne from the Delphic god,
> No print upon the grassy road
> She leaves, to instruct pursuing eyes.
> The wind that wantoned in her hair,
> And with her ruffled garments played,
> Discovered in the flying maid,
> All that the gods e'er made, if fair.

Chloris' shock is produced not by her lover's violence but by his impotence. Thus the new context encourages the reader to see the attractions of her dishevelled form in flight as a deliberate attempt to arouse Lysander. This consciously topsy-turvy allusion to the fleeing Daphne is all the more edgy because we have already learnt that Chloris had earlier feigned reluctance when Lysander made his first advance. In fact her words seem unequivocally those of a potential rape victim:

> She cry'd – cease cease – your vain desire,
> Or I'll call out – What would you do?
> My dearer honour ev'n to you
> I cannot, must not give – Retire,
> Or take this life …

But the narrator assures us that she is only acting:

> She with a charming languishment,
> Permits his force, yet gently strove;

Ovid

> Her hands his bosom softly meet,
> But not to put him back design'd,
> Rather to draw him on inclin'd.

Chloris assumes the Daphne role so effortlessly as almost to cast doubt on the 'real' Daphne, and indeed on other rape victims. It is notoriously difficult for an outsider to distinguish between rape and consensual sex. Seen from a distance, the action the poem describes would probably suggest a male attack on an unwilling female. If the poet were male we might say that he was trivialising sexual violence, misreading genuine opposition as affected coyness. Because she is female we respond to the poem differently, perhaps uncovering a suggestion that women are forced to feign a reluctance they do not feel because of society's sexual double standards.

Although some of the more recent female responses to the poem similarly see Daphne as a victim of sexual repression, others seem to approve her self-sufficiency. Alice Fulton plays with the 'date rape' problem, but her treatment of the myth is actually more reassuring than Behn's because such a gulf yawns between Apollo (speaking below) and the poet's own voice:

> *Your presence pursues its own undoing.*
> *Just asking for it: Just use two hands and twist.*
> *As it is as it is: your femaleness naturally*
> *says take. Says this rape has your name on it.*
> *Your beauty provokes*
> *Its own dominion, whose no can never mean no.*

The italics effect a final distancing between this voice and Fulton's own – when her Daphne says no, she means it. Fulton

1. Daphne

imaginatively probes Daphne's motives; her nymph's fantastical perspective on words and objects, and particularly her conflation of literal and metaphorical spaces, recalls the voice of another solitary female, the nineteenth-century American poet, Emily Dickinson. Fulton's Daphne sees marriage itself as a kind of metamorphosis, one which offers her less freedom than transformation into a laurel:

> But her gift for visualizing the inner
> chambers
> of words was most impressive. She'd tell of *wedlock's* wall
> that was a shroud
> of pink, its wall that was a picket fence, the one of chainlink
> and one
> that was all strings. While Apollo hardened with love for her,
> Daphne
> stripped the euphemism from the pith. *Love* was nothing
> but a suite
> of polished steel: mirrors breeding mirrors in successions
> of forever, his
> name amplified through sons of sons and coats of arms,
> her limbs
> spidering, her mind changed to moss and symbol, a trousseau of
> fumed wood,
> the scent of perforations as his relief rose above her
> smoky field.

However, some of the many modern women poets who have been drawn to Daphne think her determination to flee the god misjudged. In Anne Sexton's 'Where I live in this honorable house of the laurel' the nymph's treelike state is shown to be unnatural, even grotesque, and at odds with her belated stirrings of desire:

Ovid

> I live in my wooden legs and O
> my green green hands.
> too late
> to wish I had not run from you, Apollo,
> blood moves still in my bark bound veins.
> I, who ran nymph foot to root in flight,
> have only this late desire to arm the trees
> I lie within.

The reference to 'wooden legs' rather than a trunk conjures up a clumsy Pinocchio-like image, less graceful yet more human than a fully laurelled Daphne. Throughout the poem, language itself is subjected to Ovidian metamorphosis; the O at the end of line one is linked syntactically with the wooden legs as though it too were somehow part of her physical environment. Even though the next line shows O to be an exclamation, the misreading is not without significance as the letter traditionally connotes female genitalia – a kind of absent presence for this yearning Daphne – and here may also suggest her new shape, the ring of a tree. Her memory of being transformed into a laurel is reflected in the confused syntax of 'I, who ran nymph foot to root in flight'. A single letter metamorphoses her 'foot' into a 'root', encouraging us to see both words as the same part of speech. Yet it is possible to see 'root' not as a noun but as a verb; Daphne is paradoxically rooted while 'in flight' because transformation is the only way she can escape Apollo.

The textuality – remember the Latin wordplay linking bark and foliage with books – of Daphne is also hinted at by Sexton when the speaker tells us:

> Frost taps my skin and I stay glossed
> in honor for you are gone in time.

1. Daphne

'Glossed' might signify her shining beauty, but equally suggests interpretation, and perhaps misinterpretation, for yet again we are wrongfooted by the following line, at first assuming that she is glossed in honour of the god, then realising that there is a pause after honour, and that the god seems to have vanished from the picture completely – 'you are gone in time'. It would therefore seem that her honour is entirely self-contained, her chastity rather than her gift to poets. The prominence of honour here – the tree is described as 'honorable' in the title, and the word is used three times in the poem – is significant. Its resonance continues to shift throughout the poem; her 'laureate' honour appears an empty and frustrating gift:

> I build the air with the crown of honor; it keys
> my out of time and luckless appetite.

But in the next line 'honor' seems to have metamorphosed into the honour done by Apollo to Daphne by his great desire for her:

> You gave me honor too soon, Apollo ...

Whereas Fulton sees marriage as a delusive trap, it seems that Sexton sees Daphne's fetishistic concern with her chastity as equally destructive, a position apparently shared by Sylvia Plath who also, though with some equivocation, deprecates the need to seek refuge from sexuality in metamorphosis. In 'Virgin in a Tree' she equates approval for Daphne's decision with Hamlet's wish for Ophelia to enter a nunnery:

> Here's the parody of that moral mousetrap
> Set in the proverbs stitched on samplers

Ovid

Approving chased girls who get them to a tree
And put on bark's nun-black

Habit which deflects
All amorous arrows.

Plath's vision of Daphne resembles that of Sexton, for both see the nymph's metamorphosis as grotesque and unnatural:

She, ripe and unplucked, 's
Lain splayed too long in the tortuous boughs: overripe
Now, dour-faced, her fingers
Stiff as twigs, her body woodenly
Askew ...

It is scarcely surprising that Daphne is an ambiguous figure for most modern Western women, who are likely to sympathise with her wish for independence and her refusal to subordinate her own feelings to those of her father and suitor, but find her preoccupation with virginity alienating. Daphne's retreat from sexual experience may (arguably) damage her, but leaves her tormentor unpunished. By contrast, as we shall see in the next chapter, Apollo's sister Diana responds with unforgiving violence as soon as her chastity comes under threat.

2

Actaeon

'You know the rules for a Particicution,' Aunt Lydia says. 'You will wait until I blow the whistle. After that, what you do is up to you, until I blow the whistle again. Understood?'
    A noise comes from among us, a formless assent ...
    'This man,' says Aunt Lydia, 'has been convicted of a rape.' Her voice trembles with rage, and a kind of triumph ...
    There's a surge forward, like a crowd at a rock concert in the former time, when the doors opened, that urgency coming like a wave through us. The air is bright with adrenalin, we are permitted anything and this is freedom, in my body also, I'm reeling, red spreads everywhere ... now there are sounds, gasps, a low noise like growling, yells and the red bodies tumble forward and I can no longer see, he's obscured by arms, fists, feet. A high scream comes from somewhere, like a horse in terror.
    Margaret Atwood, *The Handmaid's Tale*, 1986

Following the car crash which killed Diana, Princess of Wales, both the poet Andrew Motion and the Princess' brother, Earl Spencer, observed the same irony in her fate. Although named after the virgin goddess of the chase, she was hounded to death, the hunted, not the hunter:

> And you? Your life was not your own to keep
> or lose. Beside the river, swerving under ground,
> your future tracked you, snapping at your heels:
> Diana, breathless, hunted by your own quick hounds.
>   Andrew Motion

Ovid

My own and only explanation is that genuine goodness is threatening to those at the opposite end of the moral spectrum. It is a point to remember that of all the ironies about Diana, perhaps the greatest was this – a girl given the name of the ancient goddess of hunting was, in the end, the most hunted person of the modern age.

Earl Spencer's funeral oration

But both men's words generate as well as describe irony. For the Ovidian reader any reference to the poignancy of a hunter killed by his or her own hounds suggests a story in which Diana is the aggressor rather than the victim – the metamorphosis of Actaeon. The young prince, having finished hunting for the morning, stumbled upon Diana bathing in a grove. She sprinkled water over him, transforming him into a deer. He tried to run away but was tracked and killed by his hunting dogs. Any echo of this particular legend in Earl Spencer's speech is probably fortuitous, but it seems actually embedded within Motion's poem because of the phrase 'your own quick hounds'. This has the effect of undercutting the poem's poignant tribute by reminding us how ruthless the mythical Diana could be. It also, within the context of the Princess' life, hints that she was partly responsible for the accident. By describing the photographers and journalists as her 'own quick hounds' Motion suggests that she had previously found them useful, and exploited their hunting instinct for the purposes of self-promotion.

These ironies may have been unintentional but they are perfectly consistent with the complex reception of this legend. Much of the story's haunting energy derives from its ambiguous handling of blame and responsibility. Ovid's own version of the myth is conspicuously favourable to Actaeon, and he describes

2. Actaeon

the hunter's final metamorphosis and death with great pathos, emphasising the gulf between his animal shape and human mind. David Slavitt offers a particularly effective translation of this scene:

> His ears are sharpening into pointed
> excrescences, while his hands are pointing, becoming hoofs,
> and his arms are turning to forelegs. His skin is a hide, and his heart
> is cold with terror.

The catalogue of change cheats us into expecting that Actaeon's heart has also become something different – the placement of 'heart' at the end of the line delays and intensifies our shock when we realise that his consciousness remains that of a suffering human. This is the key to the tale's horror – the hunter fully shares the reader's awareness of his fate's terrible irony.

Ovid's sympathy for Actaeon is apparent from the very beginning of the story, for as soon as he is introduced we are assured that his fate was completely undeserved (3.141-2):

> But if you examine the facts carefully, you will find that the fault was fortune's, not Actaeon's. For how can simple bad luck be anyone's fault?

But it could be countered that the narrating voice is protesting too much – and that we are in fact being encouraged to wonder whether Actaeon was more blameworthy than Ovid's retelling suggests. Certainly some earlier versions cast him in a more dubious light – suggesting that he hid in order to spy on Diana or that he arrogantly challenged her to a hunting match, for example. At the end of Ovid's narrative a 'vox pop' invites us to think further about the goddess' behaviour (3.253-5):

> People were divided in their response. To some the goddess seemed unjustly cruel, others praise her, saying the deed befitted her stern virginity.

It is especially difficult to adjudicate between the two because they have so much in common. Both are hunters, both seek rest, weary from the chase. That their apparent opposition conceals a great affinity is perhaps suggested by the description of Diana's grotto. Here two opposites, Nature and Art, come together and cannot be distinguished from one another (3.157-60):

> In its deepest recesses was a shady grotto, worked by no artist's skill. But Nature had imitated Art using her own wit, for she had constructed a native arch of the living rock and soft tufa.

If Diana is ruthless and bloodthirsty, so is Actaeon, whose wholesale slaughter of countless animals is particularly emphasised by Ovid. (Though it is difficult to know whether the poet would have seen Actaeon's passion for hunting as problematic, just as it is difficult to know whether he meant the vegetarian Pythagoras to seem admirable or ridiculous.) It has been suggested that Diana's cruelty in Ovid is less capricious than first appears. She can be seen as a reader of her own text whose instincts have been trained on story after story of helpless females – Daphne, Io, Syrinx, Callisto – being pursued, even raped, by male predators. Thus she acts in self-defence, mistakenly assuming Actaeon's intrusion is intentional and violent.

But a reader who is trying to weigh up the balance of blame in the legend may feel that this explanation lets Diana off the

2. Actaeon

hook too easily – the theory might in any case be turned on its head by focusing less on gender and more on power. The pattern established in the first few books of the *Metamorphoses* is one of predatory deity and reluctant mortal. Might not the relationship between Diana and Actaeon retain this pattern of predation?

There is a great emphasis in the tale on Actaeon's loss of all capacity for speech. John Heath notes that 'Actaeon's muteness is uniquely severe, prolonged, and even inappropriate' (72). A clue to the reason for Diana's silencing of Actaeon might be found in the story of Philomela, which I discuss in more detail in the next chapter. Like Actaeon she is deliberately silenced whereas other characters such as Io suffer muteness as a chance byproduct of metamorphosis. As only Diana and her nymphs witnessed what really happened – apart from Actaeon whose inability to communicate we are so insistently reminded of – might not the real story be hidden from us? With her reputation for perfect chastity to protect, Diana may be trying to conceal the same secret as Tereus, a sexual encounter between herself and her mute victim. After all, if Diana was so anxious to stop anyone knowing that Actaeon had seen her naked, why is this story, in the form we have it, allowed to leak out at all? Perhaps because this version of events, in which she is portrayed as virtuous, though cruel, is one she wants bruited as widely abroad as possible.

Ovid here and elsewhere encourages us to think about the 'narrating instance', in other words the circumstances surrounding the production of his stories, their internal audiences and the motivation for their telling, and he frequently invites us to reflect on the effect of these circumstances on the way stories are told. (Think back to how – and why – Jupiter related the tale of Lycaon.) An accusation of rape is a tried and tested excuse for

Ovid

a lynching – the heroine of *The Handmaid's Tale* later discovers that the unfortunate 'rapist' she helped to murder (in the passage quoted at the beginning of this chapter) was really a political prisoner. Reading the tale of Actaeon as an elaborate cover-up may be fanciful, but this myth's afterlife is characterised by a suspicion that there is more to the tale than meets the eye, and a determination to reveal its hidden meanings.

The difficulties posed by the story for the reader who wants to come down on one side or the other make Diana a potent tool with which to register equivocation. Four centuries before Motion's edgy poem of praise for the Princess of Wales, the representation of another powerful royal was rendered ambiguous by the Actaeon myth. Addressing her as 'Cynthia' (another name for Diana), Edmund Spenser invites Elizabeth I to find her reflection in his epic masterpiece *The Faerie Queene* (3 Proem 5):

> Ne let his fairest Cynthia refuse,
> In mirrours more then one her selfe to see,
> But either Gloriana let her chuse,
> Or in Belphoebe fashioned to bee:
> In th'one her rule, in th'other her rare chastitee.

As well as explicitly identifying two characters as incarnations of Elizabeth (Gloriana and Belphoebe) Spenser's address to the Queen as Cynthia/Diana tacitly alerts us to the possible significance of allusions to Diana in the poem. The story of Actaeon – with its emphasis on the goddess' majesty, virginity and sharp temper – would have been a particularly resonant episode for a readership of Elizabethan courtiers. However, whether or not Spenser was alert to the possible effect he was creating, the first echo of the myth (in Book 1) is by no means complimentary to Elizabeth-as-Diana.

2. Actaeon

Immediately after the Red Cross Knight has encountered the wicked enchantress Duessa he plucks a bough from a tree, causing it to bleed, and learns that the tree is in fact a metamorphosed man, Fraudubio. The speaking tree describes how he was himself bewitched by Duessa's seeming beauty before discovering the deception (1.2.40-1):

> Till on a day (that day is every prime)
> When witches wont do penance for their crime)
> I chaunst to see her in her proper hew,
> Bathing her selfe in origane and thyme:
> A filthy foule old woman I did vew,
> That ever to haue toucht her, I did deadly rew.
> Her neather partes misshapen, monstruous,
> Were hidd in water, that I could not see,
> But they did seeme more foule and hideous,
> Then womans shape man would beleeue to bee ...

It is not only the reference to a man's unintentional glimpse of a bathing female which signals an Actaeon link. Apparently a gulf separates the ugly witch Duessa from the beautiful goddess Diana. But this gulf would be closed for readers who were aware of the lively, scurrilous explanation for Diana's fury offered by the Greek satirist Lucian:

> She made them worry him for fear
> He should tell tales, and blaze a story
> (She knew must needs be detractory)
> Of what a filthy fulsome quean,
> He bathing had stark naked seen.
> For the virginity (forsooth)
> She brags of, is a gross untruth ...

Ovid

Both Lucian's Diana and Spenser's Duessa seek to protect their reputations for beauty and chastity by metamorphosing their unwitting spies. We may imagine that the reflex which drove Lucian to transform Diana from a beautiful virgin into a misshapen crone must have found a parallel within real life – a queen who vaunted her own, slightly suspect, virginity, who insisted on being treated as a beauty despite her advancing years, and whose popularity was on the wane, must have been a tempting target for satirists.

When we encounter the 'real' Diana in Book 3 of *The Faerie Queene*, the apparently straightforward account of the bathing goddess being disturbed by the advent of Venus may be tainted by our memories of Duessa (3.6.19):

> Soone as she *Venus* saw behind her backe,
> She was asham'd to be so loose surprized,
> And woxe halfe wroth against her damzels slacke,
> That had not her thereof before avized,
> But suffred her so carelesly disguized
> Be ouertaken ...

'Loose' ostensibly refers to her state of undress, but is commonly used to signify wanton, as when Spenser describes Red Cross's dream of Una transformed into a 'loose leman' (48). And although 'disguized' may be glossed 'undressed', the alternative meanings of 'concealed' and 'deformed' were also available in the Renaissance, harking back to Lucian's interpretation of the tale.

Ovid had already set a precedent for equating Diana with an irascible and unforgiving ruler, a response to the tale which would become far more potent for writers whose monarch was both female and, supposedly, virginal. In his later exile poetry, Ovid cast Augustus as Diana and identified himself with Actaeon,

2. Actaeon

claiming that both he and Actaeon were innocent victims of chance, and thus suggesting that the mysterious error for which he was relegated involved some chance discovery of scandal. Ovid's seventeenth-century translator, George Sandys, confirmed such a reading of the tale when he explained that the myth can be taken to show 'how dangerous a curiosity it is to search into the secrets of Princes, or by chance to discover their nakednesse: who thereby incurring their hatred ever after live the life of a Hart, full of feare and suspicion'.

Ovid's creation of a link between his own unwitting error and the hunter's mistake has not necessarily made interpretation of Actaeon's story any more straightforward for the commentators of later centuries. For Ovid himself is a kind of mythical figure – as ambiguous as any character in the *Metamorphoses* – and as subject to the vagaries of interpretation. One uncanny story describes how two clerics prayed for Ovid's soul by his tomb, only for the poet's disembodied voice to speak out, rejecting Christ and salvation. Another tradition, by contrast, holds that he was converted to Christianity and became St Naso, Bishop of Tomis. So it is not surprising that we find medieval interpreters explaining the story of his alter ego Actaeon in diametrically opposed ways. Some said that Actaeon was really an idle and extravagant youth who lost his entire fortune through keeping expensive hounds, while others associated Actaeon with Christ. With rather Ovidian ingenuity, commentators linked the hunter's metamorphosis into a stag – 'cerf' in French – with Christ's incarnation as a man, the 'suffering servant' of Isaiah, or serf.

A further comic, secular approach to Actaeon's story focused on his acquisition of horns. It would seem that for readers and audiences in the sixteenth, seventeenth and eighteenth centuries, jokes about cuckolds – traditionally associated with horns – were irresistibly and inexplicably hilarious. It is not entirely clear why horns were associated with cuckolds, although it has been suggested that the joke derives from the practice of distinguishing capons from cockerels by grafting their spurs onto their combs. Here they apparently grew as 'horns'. As a castrated cockerel, the capon had an affinity with the supposedly 'unmanned' cuckold. With predictable misogyny it was even sometimes claimed that Diana, although reputed chaste, in fact cuckolded Actaeon:

> The first of the three,
> Diana should be,
> But she cuckolded poor Actæon,
> And his head she adorns,
> With such visible horns,
> That he's fit for his hounds for to prey on.

Thus Alexander Brome (a Restoration poet) metamorphoses Diana, like Daphne, from a virgin into a whore.

In Shakespeare's *Twelfth Night* the lovesick Duke Orsino seems to shift the blame away from the goddess when he casts the beautiful Olivia as Diana and himself as Actaeon (1.1.18-21):

> O, when mine eyes did see Olivia first
> Methought she purged the air of pestilence;
> That instant was I turned into a hart,
> And my desires like fell and cruel hounds,
> E'er since pursue me.

For Orsino the hounds have been internalised as his own self-destructive desires, and the pun on 'heart' and 'hart' suggests that any metamorphosis he has undergone (by contrast with

2. Actaeon

Ovid's version of events) transforms his mind rather than his body. Although his words imply no conscious cruelty on Olivia's part – she did not intend to affect him in this way – it could be argued that, simply by invoking the myth, he subtly implies that she is to blame for not returning his love. The impact of her indifference is as great as that of Diana's fury.

A similar reading of the myth is implied when the mysterious and beautiful Ayesha in Rider Haggard's *She* (1887) warns the hero, Holly, that it would be dangerous for him to behold her dazzling beauty:

> 'Was there not one Actæon who perished miserably because he looked on too much beauty? If I show thee my face, perchance thou wouldst perish miserably also; perchance thou wouldst eat out thy heart in impotent desire; for know I am not for thee – I am for no man, save one, who hath been, but is not yet.'

Although her allusion implies that Diana was innocent of any harmful intent, Ayesha is as cruel and pitiless as Ovid's goddess, and her final metamorphosis from an ageless beauty to a shrivelled crone links her with the Lucianic anti-Diana tradition.

The interpretation of Actaeon's death as a kind of self-consummation by one's own desires works in non-sexual contexts too. Robinson Jeffers, writing in the early twentieth century, uses Actaeon's fate as a metaphor for man's projected self-destruction through science:

> Man, introverted man, having crossed
> In passage and but a little with the nature of things this latter century
> Has begot giants; but being taken up

Ovid

> Like a maniac with self-love and inward conflicts cannot
>   manage his hybrids.
> Being used to deal with edgeless dreams,
> Now he's bred knives on nature turns them also inward: they
>   have thirsty points though.
> His mind forebodes his own destruction;
> Actaeon who saw the goddess naked among leaves and his
>   hounds tore him.
> A little knowledge, a pebble from the shingle,
> A drop from the oceans: who would have dreamed this infi-
>   nitely little too much?

Actaeon seems to morph into Victor Frankenstein here, the hunter's fragments reassembled as the overreaching scientist.

Perhaps simply because the responses to the Actaeon myth which have come down to us are, by definition, produced by literary men and women, one strand of the story's reception associates the voracious hounds with literary parasites. The Cavalier poet, Sir John Denham, describes the Jacobean playwright John Fletcher as an Actaeon murdered by imitators who stole his ideas while Thomas Mathias, writing at the end of the eighteenth century, exclaims:

> Must I for Shakspeare no compassion feel,
> Almost eat up by commentating zeal?

He parodies Ovid's long catalogue of hounds, reinventing them as Shakespeare's hordes of commentators, before concluding:

> Hot was the chace; I left it out of breath;
> I wish'd not to be in at Shakspeare's death.

Aptly, in the context of a myth which makes it difficult for us to know which side we should be on, the poet is himself impli-

2. Actaeon

cated in the slaughter of Actaeon-as-Shakespeare. The narrator is out of breath – he may not have been in at the kill, but he has certainly been running in the hunt. And, in writing this poem, Mathias in a sense becomes part of the critical tradition he satirises.

Much of the myth's power lies in its invocation of a mysterious taboo. A single unwitting step seals Actaeon's fate, and the disproportionate nature of his punishment makes the reader struggle to find some hidden meaning behind Diana's action. The mysterious, nebulous taboo attached to Diana's grove encourages us to extrapolate some more specific prohibition. One website I stumbled across while hunting for Actaeon texts was guarded with a warning of the kind Actaeon himself could have done with: 'if you don't know exactly why you're here you probably shouldn't be'. I trespassed far enough into the site to learn a new word, 'zoophilia'. Actaeon's metamorphic status between beast and human was being used to encode one of society's strongest taboos. Although the focus of this site was apparently rather remote from the original legend, there is a precedent for reinventing the Actaeon myth as the tale of a sexual liaison between beast and human (or goddess).

Whereas the website in question warned me not to progress further if I was under 18, primary school children everywhere receive their first exposure to Shakespeare through *A Midsummer Night's Dream*. Here Titania (as Diana is called by Ovid in the Actaeon story) has a sexual liaison with Bottom after he has been given an ass's head by Puck and has crossed the threshold from the mortal to the fairy world. As Thomas Boehrer arrestingly contends: 'Although no one has paid much sustained attention to the fact, *A Midsummer Night's Dream* is patently about bestiality.' He explains that Oberon purposely drugs Titania in order to ensure her sexual bondage to a beast as a way of reinforcing marital authority. And certainly in one of the play's principal sources, *The Golden Ass*, a novel by the Roman writer Apuleius about a man, Lucius, who is transformed into a donkey, much lewd attention is paid to the protagonist's erotic appeal to humans of both sexes. Significantly, the story of Actaeon is a potent intertext in *The Golden Ass* – Lucius is turned into a donkey after spying on the witch Pamphile.

Another curious eroticisation (and reversal) of the myth can be found in an early work of Boccaccio, *La Caccia di Diana*, in which a long and appreciative description of Diana hunting with her beautiful attendants concludes when Venus intervenes and turns all the hunted deer into handsome young men who pair off with the nymphs. A twist is provided by the poem's final revelation – that the voyeuristic narrator is himself a stag who will be rewarded with one of the nymphs he had admired, even though (as we only now realise) he was their natural prey.

This link between eroticism and hunting should not really surprise us. As seen in the previous chapter, a man pursuing a woman is often compared to a predator chasing its prey. The tendency to link hunting and sex together in our minds is apparent from many of the expressions we use. Someone who pursues his or her loved one obsessively is a 'stalker'; sexually promiscuous men are called 'wolves' or 'lady-killers' – neither term necessarily implying disapproval. The tale of Little Red Riding Hood seems to be about the dangers of being eaten up by a wolf, but its real message is probably a warning against sexual predators.

This erotic potential of the hunt is exploited by Shakespeare in a poem based on another Ovidian story, *Venus and Adonis*. The sexual reversal of the erotic chase – Venus pursues the beautiful but reluctant youth Adonis – is mirrored in the reversal

2. Actaeon

which brings about Adonis' death – the hunted boar becomes the hunter and gores Adonis with his tusks. His death suggests a further inversion: rather than an active male wooer he is the passive object of the boar's desire, which is expressed in unambiguously homoerotic language (1115-16):

> And, nuzzling in his flank, the loving swine
> Sheathed unaware the tusk in his soft groin.

The same sense of violent death in a hunt replacing or figuring an expected sexual encounter seems present in C.H. Sisson's free translation of the Actaeon story:

> To show her bitter virgin spite
> There was some blood but not her own.

The potential equivalence between sex and death, signalled within a Roman context by the similarity of *mors* and *amor* and within a Renaissance context by the slang use of 'death' to mean sexual climax, is here allowed to emerge through the reminder that sex between Actaeon and the virginal Diana would also have resulted in bloodshed.

Bestiality is not the only sexual taboo associated with the Actaeon story. Although the dynamic of the legend, in so far as it is sexual at all, seems heterosexual, it is amenable to queering of different kinds. In particular, the strong sense of transgression or boundary-crossing inherent in the myth may figure same-sex desire even though it is concealed behind a male/female encounter. (It is quite common for different kinds of taboos to stand for one another – for example in many texts a symbolic link is forged between cannibalism and incest.)

Aphra Behn reanimates the legend in 'Verses to a Fair Lady

that desired she would absent herself, to cure her love' by casting herself as Actaeon and the lady as Diana. Both the forbidden territory and the goddess' fury gain new significance within a context of unrequited lesbian love. The playwright Christopher Marlowe had earlier given Diana, rather than Actaeon, a sex change. When, in *Edward II*, the king's lover Gaveston describes the wanton entertainments he will devise to amuse Edward, it is the story of Actaeon and Diana, with its sexually charged atmosphere of danger and transgression, rather than some more obviously erotic narrative, which he translates into a homoerotic context (1.1.60-9):

> Sometime a louelie boye in *Dians* shape,
> With haire that gilds the water as it glides,
> Crownets of pearle about his naked armes,
> And in his sportfull hands an Oliue tree,
> To hide those parts which men delight to see,
> Shall bathe him in a spring, and there hard by,
> One like Actæon peeping through the groue,
> Shall by the angrie goddesse be transformde,
> And running in the likenes of an Hart,
> By yelping hounds puld downe, and seeme to die.

The literal and metaphorical resonances of tabooed ground are brought into still closer conjunction by Camille Paglia. According to the explanation of the legend which she offers in her online advice column, Actaeon is destroyed because he witnesses tabooed behaviour – sexual contact between Diana and her handmaidens: 'The forbidden allure of watching nude women cavort with one another can be detected as early as the Greek myth of Actaeon, the hunter who spied on the goddess Artemis bathing with her nymphs. She didn't take it very well:

2. Actaeon

She turned him into a stag torn to pieces by his own hounds, which symbolise his lecherous desires.' Paglia's reading of the legend is a playful response to a male correspondent who is confused by his voyeuristic attraction to lesbianism. But the reception of another Ovidian tale, that of Philomela, confirms the readiness of readers to associate violent vengeance taken against men with lesbian sexuality, as well as the impulse to forge links between apparently quite distinct forms of tabooed behaviour.

3
Philomela

Tereus raped Philomela and cut out her tongue,
but she wove a cape that told the story,
the voice of the shuttle, Sophocles called it.
But that's only half: her sister saw the cape and understood.
Some stories float; others are held under
until someone sees a small series of bubbles and knows
there's a body to be dredged.
          Natasha Sajé, 'Tongues', *Red Under the Skin*, 1984

We seem to accept only what is seen and what is said as evidence. These limitations have shaped both how we know and how we imagine the lesbian. I want to argue for the possibilities of the 'not said' and the 'not seen' as conceptual tools for the writing of lesbian history. Recognizing the power of not naming – of the unsaid – is a crucial means for understanding a past that is so dependent upon fragmentary evidence, gossip, and suspicion.
          Martha Vicinus (1994), 57-8

Few of Ovid's tales are more savage and painful than that of Actaeon. One of these few is the story of Philomela. This opens with the marriage of Philomela's sister Procne to King Tereus of Thrace – the match cements a military alliance between him and the girls' father, King Pandion of Athens. The wedding is ill-omened; it is attended by the Furies rather than Hymen, god of marriage. But at first all goes well, and Procne gives birth to a son, Itys. However after five years she begs Tereus to allow her to see Philomela again and he returns to Athens to request a visit. When he sees how beautiful Philomela is he becomes inflamed with love. As soon as they have landed in Thrace, Tereus drags her to a secluded hut, rapes her and cuts out her tongue so that she cannot proclaim his wickedness. But even though she is kept a prisoner Philomela contrives to let her sister know what has happened. She weaves her story onto a tapestry and smuggles it into the palace. The festival of Bacchus is being celebrated and Procne takes advantage of the atmosphere of riot and confusion to rescue Philomela. Then the sisters take a terrible revenge. They kill Procne's little son Itys, cook him and serve the dish to Tereus. When the frenzied Philomela emerges from hiding and hurls the child's head at his father, Tereus draws his sword and attempts to kill the sisters. But all three are transformed into birds, preventing further violence.

Some critics would argue that the meaning of a text is generated at the point of reception – in other words that it is the reader rather than the writer who decides what a story or poem is really about. This need not mean that anything goes, or that all readings are equally valuable. (Though the Vicinus passage quoted at the beginning of this chapter issues an irresistible challenge to be inventive!) If reading about Proserpina's fatal taste of pomegranate, which doomed her to spend six months of the year in the Underworld, puts us in mind of Eve and the apple, we are reading that myth in a way its originators could not have imagined or intended. But because the Christian tradition is so powerful in Western culture our tendency to associate the stories together is not an eccentric, isolated impulse, but a move which unites us with a whole community of readers – including Milton, who compared Eve with Proserpina in *Paradise Lost*. But if the story of Proserpina reminds us of some

3. Philomela

event from our childhood, such a reading is unlikely to have significance for anyone but ourselves.

My own most recent thoughts about Philomela's story certainly originated outside Ovid's text – they stem from research carried out for my previous book, a study of the sister relationship in nineteenth-century literature. One chapter focused on homoerotic bonds between sisters, bonds which sometimes proved more powerful than heterosexual ties. To give just one example from a well known novel, Jo March in *Little Women* tells her mother that Meg 'gets prettier every day, and I'm in love with her sometimes' and exclaims 'I just wish I could marry Meg myself, and keep her safe in the family'. I'm sure I would not have detected any hint of homoeroticism in the relationship between Philomela and Procne if I had not already been researching lesbian incest in this very different context. Certainly there is nothing in Ovid to match the sensuality of Christina Rossetti's sister heroines in 'Goblin Market':

> 'Did you miss me?
> Come and kiss me.
> Never mind my bruises,
> Hug me, kiss me, suck my juices
> Squeezed from goblin fruits for you,
> Goblin pulp and goblin dew.
> Eat me, drink me, love me;
> Laura, make much of me:
> For your sake I have braved the glen
> And had to do with goblin merchant men.'

But at least if my interpretation of the tale was ultimately a misreading, I was not quite alone in my suspicions. In Ovid the wild women-only Bacchanal which reunites the sisters is not given any special emphasis. But in Timberlake Wertenbaker's play *Love of the Nightingale* (first performed in 1988) the secret rites in which Procne participates clearly involve lesbian sexuality. The scene in which the soldiers spy on the women's rites (seen but yet not seen as they remain hidden from the audience) suggests both their sexual nature and their capacity to enrage men:

> *Second Soldier:* That window, there. We could see through the shutters.
> *First Soldier:* It's supposed to be a mystery, a woman's mystery...
> *Second Soldier:* You could sit on my shoulders. Make sure your girl's behaving.
> *First Soldier:* It's all women in there.
> *Second Soldier:* It's all men in a war.
> *First Soldier:* You mean, she – they – no.
> *Second Soldier:* Have a look.
> *First Soldier:* If she – I'll strangle her.

The window might be seen as a window onto the myth itself, hinting at a buried narrative of female sexuality which excludes men. Alternatively, Wertenbaker's importation of a lesbian undercurrent into the story could be read as an extrapolation, legitimate in a new fiction, but one which reflects late twentieth-century perceptions of female separatist behaviour and which has nothing to do with the original *Metamorphoses*. If we are unsure how to interpret Ovid's Bacchanal we might seek clues in *The Bacchae*, written by the Greek tragedian Euripides four centuries earlier. This play included a more detailed exploration of women-only rites. King Pentheus is infuriated by the introduction of a Dionysiac cult into Thebes, particularly when his own aunt and mother become involved in

3. Philomela

the excesses. Like Wertenbaker's soldiers, he is fascinated as well as appalled by their activities. When he too considers spying on the women, Dionysus tells him 'But for all your sorrow, you'd like very much to see them?' (line 815). Pentheus himself later acknowledges a prurient interest (lines 957-8):

> I can see them already, there among the bushes,
> Mating like birds, caught in the toils of love.

However, although the emphasis is on the women, it is possible that Pentheus envisions them mating with men rather than each other. An apparently more secure association between women-only worship and lesbianism can be found in Plutarch's account of a scandal which shook Rome shortly before the birth of Ovid. Clodius spied on the secret female rites of the Bona Dea, disguised as a woman, but was found out when a female devotee propositioned him. At least that is what some interpreters and commentators would have us believe. The Greek may be translated 'Aurelia came upon him and asked him to play with her, as one woman would another'. Play may signify sexual activity, but might also suggest that she wants him to play the lute. (He is disguised as a lute-girl.)

Although Euripides' play seems very different from Ovid's story, the endings are surprisingly similar, for both conclude when a boy – a youth in Euripides, a child in Ovid – is torn apart by his mother and aunt. Both narratives are preoccupied with the transgression of boundaries and the shattering of taboos. Dionysus characterises Pentheus as one who is 'curious to see forbidden sights' (912-13), and the same dangerous confusions inhere in the later Ovidian story. Tereus rapes his sister-in-law Philomela 'fassusque nefas', 'openly confessing his impious deed' (524). The English translation does not capture the jarring contradiction of this description. Tereus, Ovid informs us, speaks that which may not be spoken. Of course the apparent paradox is hardly insurmountable. To rape a defenceless girl, the sister of his wife, may be, to use an English idiom, too horrible for words, but there is nothing concrete to prevent Tereus from articulating his dreadful purpose. But 'fassusque nefas' perhaps signals a peculiarly charged tension between communication and the uncommunicable in this text. In *The Love of the Nightingale*, Timberlake Wertenbaker speculates suggestively about the narrative's secret, hidden energies (pp. 19-20):

> What is a myth? The oblique image of an unwanted truth, reverberating through time .... And what about Procne, the cause perhaps, in any case the motor of a myth that leaves her mostly absent?

One way of moving Procne back centrestage is to focus less on the direct, incestuous connection between Tereus and Philomela and more on the covert, indirectly incestuous bond between the sisters. Tereus' passion, as Philomela herself eloquently argues in Ovid, is wrong for many reasons, but particularly because it is incestuous (6.537-8):

> You have turned everything upside down. I have been made into a concubine, you a husband to us both. Now Procne must be my foe.

Although incest is a universal taboo, that which constitutes incest varies greatly from culture to culture. But Philomela's horror would have been perfectly understandable to Ovid's later Christian readers. The Bible's teaching on incest was inconsistent. Jacob married two sisters, Leah and Rachel, in

3. Philomela

turn. However Christian practice took the prohibitions listed in Leviticus 18 ('You shall not uncover the nakedness of your brother's wife, it is your brother's nakedness') as the basis for establishing prohibited degrees between relatives of affinity – in-laws.

Pace Leah and Rachel, the same prohibition was more or less strictly enforced against a woman sleeping with her sister's husband. If we invert Leviticus – 'you shall not uncover the nakedness of your sister's husband, it is your sister's nakedness' – and map its warning onto Ovid, we may view the story of Philomela in a rather different light.

Historically it is the man's predicament which has been emphasised, but it is possible to reframe this taboo in terms of the indirect sexual connection effected between sisters. In *Two Sisters and Their Mother: The Anthropology of Incest*, Françoise Héritier highlights the importance of this 'secondary' incest 'between same-sex blood relatives who are not homosexual but who share the same sexual partner' (p. 12), a liaison which implies 'an inconceivable carnal intimacy between blood relatives, expressible only by innuendo' (p. 44). She asserts that many societies would find it more acceptable for a man to sleep with his daughter than with his son's wife, for the latter act leads to an indirect homosexual liaison between father and son. Héritier concentrates on examples from non-European cultures, but asserts that these taboos have also been a powerful force in Western society. She briefly alludes to the story of Philomela as an example of this type of incest. 'Through Tereus, Philomela has committed incest with her sister' (p. 52).

If we re-examine the story in the light of Héritier's observations, Procne, 'the motor of a myth that leaves her mostly absent', regains prominence, while Tereus is less an agent of incest than a conduit for incest. For it is possible to see Tereus'

91

Ovid

rape, not as the definitive act which creates a bond between the sisters, but simply as the cementing of an existing closeness. It is after all Procne, not Tereus, who planned Philomela's visit. She asks for the visit as a favour 'cum blandita' – coaxingly or flatteringly. In Chaucer's retelling of the story in *The Legend of Good Women* rather more urgency attends the request (2260-2):

> Till on a day she gan so sore longe
> To sen hire sister, that she say nat longe
> That for desyr she niste what to seye ...

The word 'desyr' is normally used by Chaucer in a context of heterosexual passion. Here it comes unexpectedly, and is significantly attended by a temporary loss of speech. Procne seems to have no words with which to express her feelings. But in fact the very next line denies any such dumbness: 'But to hire husbonde gan she for to preye.' This little fissure in the text between *fas* and *nefas* – what can and cannot be spoken – gestures at a gap between what the myth's surface communicates and what Timberlake Wertenbaker describes as its 'unwanted truth'. If Chaucer's text hints at a 'love which dare not speak its name' on Procne's part, it would seem that his Tereus is alert to his wife's feelings. When Philomela weaves her tapestry it is in order to reveal 'How she was served for her systers love' (2365). Here we have a hint of an alternative motivation for Tereus' rage: she is the victim not of lust and a purely pragmatic, self-serving violence; she is punished for partaking in an economy of desire from which he is excluded. We may compare the urge felt by Wertenbaker's soldier to strangle his girlfriend if he finds out she's been involved in the lesbian Bacchanal.

Tereus' ardour for Philomela is controlled – ventriloquised – by Procne (6.467-71):

3. Philomela

Now he fears a delay, and eagerly repeated Procne's request, using her words to press his own case. Love gave him eloquence, and whenever he urged her more pressingly than he should have done, he asserted that Procne wished it so. He wept as well, as though Procne had asked him to.

The significance of this ventriloquism, the way he almost becomes Procne when his desire is most fiercely kindled, is heightened in an adaptation of the myth by the Elizabethan writer, George Gascoigne. Whereas Ovid's Tereus seems more or less in control of the effect he creates, deliberately invoking Procne's wishes as an excuse for ardour, Gascoigne suggests a more mysterious and elliptical relationship between the desires of husband and wife:

> Love made him eloquent
> And if he cravde too much,
> He then excusde him selfe, and saide
> That Prognes words were such.
>
> His teares confirmed all
> Teares: like to sisters teares,
> As who shuld say by these fewe drops
> Thy sisters griefe appeares.

Gascoigne's Pandion invokes an incestuous hothouse of complex shared desires. The repetition of 'desire' and 'crave' intensifies their impact and significance, and blurs the distinction between heterosexual lust and sisterly love:

> He usde this parting speech:
> Daughter (quoth he) you have desire
> Your sisters court to seech.

Ovid

> Your sister seemes likewise
> Your companie to crave,
> That crave you both, & Tereus here
> The selfe same thing would have.
>
> Ne coulde I more withstande
> So many deepe desires ...

The strength and significance of Procne's own desire for Philomela is further suggested when Gascoigne amplifies Ovid's account of Procne's original longing to see her sister. Ovid doesn't describe the desire itself, only the outcome. But Gascoigne explains how:

> Such coles of kindely love did seme
> Within hir brest to be.

So, when we later learn of Tereus' passion, his burning desire for Philomela seems but a reflex of Procne's own feelings. He mirrors her not just with his words and gestures but in his mind:

> And as the blazing bronde,
> Might kindle rotten reeds:
> Even so hir looke a secret flame,
> Within his bosome breedes.

Procne's ardour is echoed still more tellingly and startlingly at the very end of Gascoigne's poem when we learn of Tereus' fate as a henpecked hoopoe:

> As soone as *coles of kinde*
> Have warmed him to do
> The selly shift of dewties dole
> Which him belongeth to:

3. Philomela

> His hen straight way him hates,
> And flieth farre him fro,
> And close conveis hir eggs from him,
> As from hir mortal foe [my italics].

Here 'coles of kinde' unequivocally reference heterosexual congress, and strengthen retrospectively the significant intensity of those 'coles of kindely love' kindled by Philomela in Procne. The repetition is all the more significant because Gascoigne seems to encourage his readers to ponder on the related but potentially incompatible meanings of 'kind' (amiable, pertaining to kin, pertaining to sexual generation, lawful, natural) at the very beginning of the poem when he explains of Pandion that 'kinde became so kind,/ That he two daughters had.

Again and again we can find examples of the story's English translators heightening the implicit link between Procne and Tereus. To borrow an image used by Natasha Sajé in 'Tongues', quoted at the beginning of this chapter, these translations allow a few more of the story's 'bubbles' to float to the surface. For example the epigrammatic wit of Samuel Croxall's eighteenth-century translation – 'And in his wife's, he speaks his own desires' – encourages the reader to dwell on the word 'desires'. This is withheld until the end of the line, and is separated from the phrase 'his wife's'; yet by making the reader work to excavate 'Procne's desires' from syntactic ellipsis, the importance of these silenced longings is increased. This is, admittedly, a tiny if not a tenuous hint that the desires of Procne and Tereus are disturbingly similar. But another little detail, an addition to Ovid, may strengthen such an effect by encouraging us to focus on Procne's thoughts. When she begs Tereus to let her see Philomela, Croxall's Procne 'spoke the secret wishes of her breast'.

In Sandys' translation the effect of Tereus being almost possessed by Procne is heightened by an unusually literal translation of Tereus' triumphant exclamation after Pandion relents. 'Vicimus' becomes 'She's ours'. As the rhetorical plural is so much more commonplace in Latin than in English, its surprising retention at this climactic moment may signal the contamination of Tereus' supposedly spontaneous desires by those of Procne. Wertenbaker offers an interesting variation on this merging effect by staging a play within a play at the Athenian court – the story of Phaedra, smitten with desire for her stepson Hippolytus. Trying to explain his feelings to Philomela, Tereus says 'I am Phaedra'. Through Tereus' association with an incestuous female Procne is further implicated in his lust. This effect is communicated still more strongly in Ted Hughes' translation. Here, for a moment, Tereus is completely erased from the picture, for Pandion 'Surrendered at last/ To the doubled passion of his daughters'. A little earlier Hughes seems to open a curious little window up onto the myth's hidden 'unwanted truth'. The following lines are a free but fairly faithful translation of the original Latin:

> He swore Procne
> Sickened to see her sister.
> He even wept as he spoke,
>
> As if he had brought her tears with him
> As well as her pleading words.
> God in heaven, how blind men are!

But then where Ovid had written 'Tereus is credited with proper feeling, when he is in fact masterminding a wicked plot, and winning praise for a crime' (6.73-4), Hughes substitutes:

3. Philomela

> Everybody who witnessed it marvelled
> At what this man would do for his wife's sake,
> The lengths he would go to!

At first the change may not seem too significant. Hughes reminds us of Tereus' perfidy through dramatic irony whereas Ovid makes the point more directly. But the line 'God in heaven, how blind men are' now might well apply, not to Pandion's deluded courtiers, but to the apparently uxorious Tereus, and thus suggest that he is ill advised to pander to his wife's longing for Philomela. Of course such an inference seems irrelevant to the story as we have it, but might make perfect sense in relation to the myth's possible buried subtext.

A similarly counterintuitive moment can be found in John Hopkins' 1700 version of the story. He opens at the moment of Procne's request. The odd epithet 'artful fair' suggests that the requested favour is not entirely innocent:

> Five Winters now, Wing'd with their Storms, were fled,
> Since Progne first did Royal Tereus wed.
> When thus the Artful fair her suit did move,
> Urg'd, as a proof of his continu'd Love.

This hint is carried forward through the opening movement of the poem. The emphasis on Tereus' complacency implies that he is foolish, almost as though he were admitting a rival lover into the household:

> Tereus, well pleas'd, without the least Dispute,
> Commends her Fondness, and approves her suit.

But the strange implicit affinity between Procne and Tereus, their shared desire for Philomela, is made most clearly apparent by Wertenbaker. Her Philomela says of Tereus 'Why does he follow me everywhere? Even Procne left me alone sometimes.' Procne reminisces about their early companionship, a time about which Ovid of course tells us nothing (p. 7):

'How we talked. Our words played, caressed each other, our words were tossed lightly, a challenge to catch.'

Significantly the subtle eroticism of their relationship is achieved through language – thus when Wertenbaker's Tereus robs Philomela of her tongue we may associate his act with a wish to break the sisters' bond. Procne emphasises her need to speak to Philomela: 'I want to talk to her. I want her here ... I cannot talk to my husband. I have nothing to say to my son.' The suggestion that Tereus fears verbal intimacy between his wife and her sister fits in with a shift in Philomela's threat after the rape – she is less anxious to broadcast his wickedness than to share a joke about his inadequacy. She calls him 'this scarecrow dribbling embarrassed lust'. By giving Philomela such a strong voice Wertenbaker increases the significance of Tereus' urge to silence her. The act seems driven as much by irritation at her intelligence and articulacy as by the danger she poses. As in Chaucer's version of the story, Tereus' need to silence Philomela goes beyond the need to conceal his crime.

Procne's evocation of her verbal intimacy with Philomela in Wertenbaker's play may highlight a hidden conversation between Ovid's parted sisters, one that takes place beneath the surface of the text, on the boundary between speech and silence. Each sister is silenced during the course of the story. Each sister's tongue is associated with a quest for expression which fails. Philomela's 'seeks the feet of its mistress even in its death throes' (6.560). Procne, when she receives the cloth, is similarly speechless (6.583-6):

3. Philomela

Grief strikes her dumb, and her questing tongue can find no words strong enough to express her indignation. There is no room for tears, but she rushes on to confound right and wrong, her whole mind fixed on vengeance.

This odd link between the sisters' questing tongues (the same verb *quaero*, meaning to seek but also to desire, is used in each passage) means that they are joined through language (*lingua*, like 'tongue', incorporates the meaning 'language') at precisely the moment when they are robbed of speech. Their verbal and sensual connection thus defies Tereus' attempt to part and silence them.

The later stages of the story can similarly be opened up – with some difficulty in Ovid, more readily in later versions – to reveal strange new meanings. Procne's rescue of Philomela can be read as a replay of her original rape by Tereus. His action is emphasised through 'polyptoton' – the repetition of a word in a slightly different form (6.464):

Aut *rapere* et aevo *raptam* defendere bello
(Or else to ravish her and defend the rape by brutal conflict [my italics])

So is Procne's (6.598-9):

Germanamque *rapit raptaeque* insignia Bacchi
Induit
([She] seizes her sister and clothes her in the garb of a frenzied Bacchante [my italics])

Although the primary meaning of *rapio* is 'seize' rather than 'rape' the emphatic doublet *rapit raptaeque* might take us back to the myth's pivotal action, particularly as the precise meaning of *raptaeque* is not made clear until the end of the line. *Raptae* here probably needs to be glossed 'carried away by frenzy', and applied to the Bacchante, but before we know the full context there is a possibility that it is Philomela, the raped woman, who is signified by *raptae*. The rhetorical figure of polyptoton is normally used (as here) of a verbal repetition. But the echo of one rape in another (really a rescue) is a kind of narratological polyptoton. Curiously this episode, a woman rescuing her fragile, wronged sister from incarceration by a man, anticipates Wilkie Collins' *The Woman in White*, where Marian rescues her sister Laura from a madhouse in which she has been unjustly confined by her scheming husband. The connection may be a chance one, but is significant because Marian's love for Laura has been interpreted by some readers and critics as lesbian.

Procne's next action uncannily echoes Leviticus (6.604):

Oraque develat miserae pudibunda sororis
(And she unveils the shamefaced countenance of her wretched sister.)

Whether or not we agree with the Elizabethan translator of the *Metamorphoses*, Arthur Golding, that Ovid must have had access to the Bible:

What man is he but would suppose the author of this booke
The first foundation of his woorke from Moyses wryghtings tooke?

the wording proved suggestive for the tale's later imitators and translators. *Pudibunda* may mean shameful or disgraceful, but in its more positive aspect means simply bashful or modest.

3. Philomela

Croxall invests the moment with a bridal atmosphere, suppressing Ovid's discordant *miserae*:

> She strait unveil'd her blushing sister's face,
> And fondly clasped her with a close embrace.

Sandys' translation of the same moment has an oddly stuttering quality, as though he feels some nervousness about this part of the story:

> Progne with-drawes; the sacred weeds vnlos'd;
> Her wofull sisters bashfull face disclos'd:
> Falls on her neck ...

Again Philomela and Procne seem like a bride and groom. Procne's withdrawal suggests a husband sensitive to his wife's modesty, the 'sacred weeds' are Bacchic, but through Christianisation suggest a solemn sacrament, while 'bashful' is more suggestive of sweet reluctant amorous delay than of any terrible shame. These translators may be reading a marital effect into, rather than out of, Ovid. But their shared impulse is suggestive nonetheless, implying that the myth's incestuous framework, and perhaps at least some details of Ovid's own retelling, encourage us to see a quasi-sexual connection between the sisters.

The most horrific point in the story is the murder of Itys. When the sisters feed him to Tereus they forfeit their status as the story's victims and Tereus' own villainy is almost eclipsed. But might this most unnatural act mask another focus for male anxiety? Strong bonds between women might challenge patriarchal commodification of women as units of exchange and guarantors of patrilineal continuity by further excluding men from the child rearing process. Gascoigne's observations on the mating patterns of hoopoes fit particularly aptly with such an interpretation of the story:

> As soone as coles of kinde
> Have warmed him to do
> The selly shift of dewties dole
> Which him belongeth to:
>
> His hen straight way him hates,
> And flieth farre him fro,
> And close conveis hir eggs from him,
> As from hir mortal foe.

Patricia Klindienst Joplin offers a suggestive account of the scapegoating of society's female victims which the myth's bloody conclusion may obscure:

> The end of the tale represents an attempt to forestall or foreclose a moment of radical transition when dominance and hierarchy might have begun to change or to give way. Culture hides from its own sacrificial violence. The Greek imagination uses the mythic end to expel its own violence and to avoid any knowledge of the process. Patriarchal culture feels, as Tereus does, that it is asked to incorporate something monstrous when the woman returns from exile to tell her own story. But myth seeks to blame the women for the inability of the culture to allow the raped, mutilated, but newly resisting woman to return: the sisters must become force-feeders; they must turn out to be bloodthirsty. Supposedly, the sisters quickly forget their long delayed desire to be together in giving way to the wish for revenge.

Although, as we have seen, many responses to the myth help to draw away the veil, as it were, from the hidden subtext, others

3. Philomela

seek to silence Philomela still further. For example the eighteenth-century poet Elijah Fenton seems almost to transform her hatred for Tereus into love by suggesting its equivalence to his own feelings about a dead friend:

> Or softly tune thy tender Notes to mine,
> Forgetting Tereus, make my Sorrows thine.
> Now the dear Youth has left the lonely Plain,
> And is the Grief, who was the Grace, of ev'ry British Swain.

Another eighteenth-century poet, Samuel Boyce, prettifies the myth still more outrageously:

> Then pours sweet Philomel, through dulcet throat,
> The musically, melancholy, note;
> Tereus she mourns, all lonely on a thorn,
> While turtles coo a soft farewell till morn ...

This sanitisation of the story in a sense continues Tereus' work. The rape has been excised from Philomela's story. Moving forward to the twentieth century once again, it is interesting to compare a similar silencing of the inconvenient female voice in another tale of two sisters, Tennessee Williams' *A Streetcar Named Desire*. Here Blanche Dubois disrupts her sister Stella's marriage to Stanley when she comes to stay in their small, shabby apartment. Stella's affectionate care for her charismatic and demanding sister causes her to be less attentive to her husband's needs. We sense that Stanley is jealous of Blanche's hold over Stella, and his eventual rape of Blanche seems motivated more by an urge to overpower and humiliate her than by desire. When Blanche tells her sister what has happened Stella refuses to believe her, and Blanche is committed to a mental institution, silenced less horribly than Philomela, but no less effectively.

Is Tennessee Williams' play in any sense related to Ovid's story and its complex literary reception? Or are the similarities a matter of chance alone? Maybe their points of contact are determined by shared archetypes, deep structures of thought which forge the same kind of bond between Ovid and Williams as between Ovid's Proserpina and the Judeo-Christian Eve, related stories from distinct, though not unrelated, cultural traditions.

4
Arachne

Thus Tapistry of old, the Walls adorn'd,
Ere noblest Dames the artful Shuttle scorn'd:
Arachne, then, with Pallas did contest,
And scarce th' Immortal Work was judg'd the Best.
Nor valorous Actions, then, in Books were sought;
But all the Fame, that from the Field was brought,
Employ'd the Loom, where the kind Consort wrought:
Whilst sharing in the Toil, she shar'd the Fame,
And with the Heroes mixt her interwoven Name.
No longer, Females to such Praise aspire,
And seldom now We rightly do admire.
                                        Anne Finch, 1713

The many artists featured in the *Metamorphoses* are often – rather like the banished Ovid himself – presented as victims, and their productions can frequently be read as a kind of commentary on Ovid's own art. His description of the intricate maze created by Daedalus, for example, might be a description of the *Metamorphoses* itself: 'He confused the passages and led the eye astray in a tangled maze of contradictory paths' (8.160-1).

The word 'passages' translates the Latin *notas*. *Nota* can mean any kind of sign, but is most usually applied to letters, or to writing more generally. The ambiguity is retained in the translation, for 'passages' may suggest either 'corridors' or 'paragraphs'. (This is one of those examples of metaphor being so embedded in language that we cease to notice it.) Ovid concludes the description of the labyrinth with another teasing reference to his own unreliability – 'his construction was so deceptive' (168). This quality of deliberate confusion, of not allowing the reader to know which path to take, is exemplified in one of Ovid's most famous stories about artists, the tale of Arachne.

Arachne is a mortal woman of humble birth but unparalleled skill. Her weaving makes her famous throughout Lydia, and even the nymphs flock to watch her at work. Her downfall comes through pride, for when she asserts that her genius owes nothing to Minerva, patron of weaving, the goddess comes to test her disguised as a crone. When Arachne speaks slightingly of the goddess, Minerva unmasks herself; Arachne responds by boldly challenging her to a weaving contest.

Minerva's tapestry depicts a hierarchical vision of the Olympian gods in triumph and also shows the fates of some of those, like Arachne herself, presumptuous enough to doubt or challenge their authority. The subject matter of Arachne's tapestry is in some ways similar; yet she chooses, not rebellious assertive figures, but girls such as Europa and Leda, victims of the gods' lust. The goddess is furious, partly because Arachne's tapestry is perfect, partly because of its subversive subject matter, and she first destroys it and then strikes Arachne with a wooden shuttle until she hangs herself. Feeling some pity for her victim, Minerva saves her from death by metamorphosing her into a spider.

The story – and particularly the contest – has long divided the poem's readers and commentators. It is possible to identify many responses which straightforwardly condemn Arachne's pride and self-sufficiency, and her rejection of authority,

4. Arachne

particularly divine authority. Typical of this strand is 'Arachne' by the seventeenth-century poet, Alexander Ross:

> Thou that in knowledge dost excell,
> Must humble be,
> And think what on Arachne fell,
> May fall on thee:
> It was her pride did her undo,
> And pride may overthrow thee too.

But sympathetic, even partisan, supporters of Arachne are equally easy to locate. The position of Erasmus Darwin, writing in the eighteenth century, is unequivocally expressed:

> And fair Arachne with her rival loom
> Found undeserved a melancholy doom –

A review of a recent illustrated poetic retelling of the myth for children, Kate Hovey's *Arachne Speaks*, describes Hovey's response as 'distinctly modern in its sympathy for Arachne's pride in her self-taught achievements and for her lack of respect for the gods and goddesses'. This characterisation of the 'Arachnean' perspective as modern makes a lot of sense. A modern reader is probably less likely to feel instinctive distrust for the rebellious artist than, say, a Renaissance reader.

But is it more dangerous to over- or underestimate the gap between ourselves and the productions of the past? Identifying an apparent shift from a Palladian to an Arachnean perspective over the course of the last few centuries does not necessarily help us to establish an Ovidian perspective. The responses of Christian readers are likely to evince a greater respect for divine authority than may be appropriate within a classical context. A story in which a man rebels against God – such as Marlowe's *Dr Faustus* – cannot simply be mapped onto a narrative of rebellion against a classical deity. If, as many suspect, Marlowe felt a sneaking sympathy for his overreaching anti-hero, it is highly likely that Ovid might similarly have favoured Arachne. The gods of Ovid – and other classical writers – are frequently faulty and unjust. And as they constantly quarrel amongst themselves it is no sign of special impiety to have just *one* god or goddess as an enemy. Aeneas, for example, was violently opposed by Juno but aided by many other gods including his mother Venus. More significant than such generalisations about classical literature is the evidence of the *Metamorphoses* itself. There are many compelling reasons for deducing that Ovid was on Arachne's side.

Like Arachne, Ovid is an artist whose productions get him into trouble. Ovid's notorious *Art of Love* was one of the reasons why the poet was sent into exile by Augustus. Although the poem's most obvious impropriety lay in its incitement to adultery (thus flouting Augustus' commitment to 'family values'), more particularly subversive were the subtle associations made between the imperial family and the lewd strategies counselled by Ovid's knowing narrator – he recommended the porticoes of Livia and Octavia as likely pick-up joints. Like Arachne, Ovid cocked a snook at authority and suffered the consequences. Perhaps because he identified with her, he seems to describe her own tapestry with particular élan, inserting telling little details just as he does in his own representations of myths within the larger poem (6.103-7):

Arachne depicts Europa deceived by the semblance of a bull – you would think it was a real bull and real waves. The girl

4. Arachne

seems to gaze back at the land she has left, crying out to her playmates. Fearing the touch of the surging waves, she draws back her timid feet.

If Arachne's web captivates, Minerva's tapestry may alienate the reader. She depicts herself in a prominent position, beating Neptune in an earlier contest. Considering this reminder of her highly competitive nature, not to mention the bleak and violent fates of every mortal she includes on her design, it seems ironic that the finishing touch Minerva gives her work is a border of 'peaceful olive'. She is, after all, the goddess of war as well as weaving.

It is possible that such a characteristically 'modern', Arachnean, reading of the weaving contest reflects wishful thinking on the reader's part. We like underdogs, rebels and artists and we want Ovid to like them too, just as we want to feel that Chaucer's violently anti-semitic Prioress's Tale reflects her views, not his. Arachne herself provides a warning to those who would infer that, because Ovid resembles the weaver in some ways, he must therefore sympathise with her. Although she appears to be a champion of female victims, she has little in common with these lovely, defenceless girls. Arachne is not a romantic figure, but a married woman of humble birth about whose appearance we learn nothing. If she resembles anyone, she resembles the gods whom she apparently deplores. Her creative abilities take us back to the very beginning of Ovid's poem, for the way she rolls her balls of wool echoes the description of the creator of the world moulding the earth into a ball. And the deceptive brilliance of her tapestry is equalled only by the transformative – and equally deceptive – skill of the shapeshifting gods. When he describes her depiction of Europa's rape by Jupiter disguised as a bull Ovid admiringly comments: 'you would think it was a real bull and real waves'. It is significant that he shifts position almost imperceptibly, first praising the ingenuity of Jupiter, then the wit of the weaver. Whatever Ovid's position vis-à-vis Arachne may be, it would seem that Arachne is of Jupiter's party without knowing it.

If we fail to notice the divide between Ovid's two very different expressions of praise, this is a clue to yet another link between his art and Arachne's. The hues of the tapestry shade into one another so subtly that, even though 'the extremes are clearly distinct' (67), 'the transitions between them deceive the eye' (66). This is true of Ovid's art too, not just in the little local instance noted above, but in the poem more generally. Each story shimmers confusingly into the next.

Many of the *Metamorphoses*' readers have, whether consciously or unconsciously, picked up on the possible bond between Ovid and Arachne and reinvented it in their own responses to the poem. A striking example is Velazquez's painting of the myth, *Las Hilenderas* or *The Spinners*. This seems to depict different stages of the story: the contest between Arachne and Minerva (still disguised as a crone) dominates the foreground while the tale's denouement is shown on a more distant plane behind them. The more remote Arachne – the figure in the background – has an uncertain status. She seems neither more nor less 'real' than Europa, as depicted by Velazquez on the painted tapestry, just as within the *Metamorphoses* itself both Arachne and Europa are equally fictive. In creating this effect Velazquez also encourages us to draw a parallel between his own art and the mythical weaver's: we cannot tell where his painting ends and her tapestry begins.

Shakespeare similarly inscribes himself as Arachne at the end

4. Arachne

of *Troilus and Cressida*. Troilus has just witnessed Cressida faithlessly transfer her affections from him to Diomede. He cannot believe that this is the same woman he loved:

> ... this is, and is not, Cressid.
> Within my soul there doth conduce a fight
> Of this strange nature that a thing inseparate
> Divides more wider than the sky and earth,
> And yet the spacious breadth of this division
> Admits no orifex for a point as subtle
> As Ariachne's broken woof to enter.

Cressida has a double nature though a single self; the speech is elliptical but may be illuminated if we remember Ovid's account of Arachne working from one extreme of the colour spectrum to the other, but so subtly that we barely notice the change from one shade to the next. Her art resembles Shakespeare's in so far as Cressida too confounds us, and Troilus, by her shifting nature. The name Ariachne is a strange conflation of Arachne with Ariadne – also associated with skilful handling of wool, through her contrivance of the clew which allows Theseus to escape from the labyrinth. Although almost certainly a slip – either Shakespeare's or the compositor's – this new woven name, like Cressida's character, like Arachne's web, is another 'thing inseparate', single and yet divisible.

Another telling example of a writer aligning himself with Arachne comes in the translation of the *Metamorphoses* used by Shakespeare, Golding's version of 1547. He explains that Minerva 'purposed to put the Lydian Maide/ Arachne to hir neckeverse.' This curious expression is defined by the Oxford English Dictionary as follows:

Ovid

> A Latin verse printed in black-letter (usually the beginning of the fifty-first psalm) formerly set before one claiming benefit of clergy ... by reading which he might save his neck.

By proving his ability to translate Latin, a felon demonstrated that he had received clerical training and thus had a right to 'benefit of clergy' – that is, he was exempt from trial by a secular court. The poet and playwright Ben Jonson, among others, benefited from this bizarre legal loophole. Golding's use of the phrase seems a curiously naïve anachronism, yet on further inspection generates a complexly Ovidian charge. In using a specifically English word pertaining to Christian customs entirely alien to the classical world of the *Metamorphoses*, Golding replicates Ovid's own fondness for Romanising touches. We tend to forget that the gap which separated Ovid from his earliest Greek sources is far greater than that which separates us from Shakespeare and Golding. So when Ovid says that Cyparissus' pet stag wears a *bulla* – a specifically Roman symbol of freeborn status – he creates an effect every bit as incongruous as Golding's reference to the 'neckeverse'.

Returning to Arachne herself, it might be noted that there is a further incongruity involved in putting her to her neckeverse, for few English women could pass such a test and – because women could not of course be ordained – none would ever be given the opportunity to qualify for 'benefit of clergy'. But, although doubly incongruous, the expression is of course apt because Arachne does hang by the neck. And thus we are encouraged to dwell on the unfairness of Minerva's approach. 'Putting someone to one's neckeverse' is a challenge to show skill. Arachne passed this test conspicuously well. Yet she is constructively executed, as it were, all the same.

Having shown that Golding's odd use of the term 'neckeverse'

4. Arachne

works on Arachne's behalf, I would like to suggest that it also forges a very specific link between her and Golding. The skills tested by the 'neckeverse' challenge were literary/linguistic rather than artistic. One might thus say that Golding is acknowledging and bringing out Arachne's link with her creator Ovid. But, still more specifically, the felon needed to prove his ability to translate from Latin, precisely the skill Golding demonstrates in his *Metamorphoses*. Perhaps through this move Golding situates Ovid on Minerva's side, as the figure of authority and tradition with whom the modern writer competes at his peril.

Both the Latin and English languages make associations between weavers and poets especially easy and apt. We connect the two arts together, probably without realising it, whenever we talk about spinning yarns, weaving the threads of a plot, or effecting a denouement. The Romans similarly elided the two activities, as did the Greeks – the word rhapsode, meaning poet, was etymologically linked to weaving. Poets drawing on the Arachne myth instinctively exploited this shared terminology, associating their craft with her web. The Elizabethan poet Thomas Storer self-deprecatingly explains that his poem is no great work of art:

> But rather such a web as I could frame
> In slender lines, yet slender as they be,
> My Muse *Arachne*-like presents to thee.

In the early nineteenth century Lady Emmeline Stuart-Wortley disassociated herself from those who 'weave a dazzling web of words,/ Subtle as those Arachne wove'. So interwoven are the arts of weaving and literature that we are unlikely to remember (or indeed know) that the primary meaning of 'subtle' is 'finely woven' and that it derives from a Latin verb *subtexo*, to weave under.

Stuart-Wortley's implied slight distrust of Arachnean subtlety connects with another important strand in the story's reception, one well described by Jonathan Sawday (2000, p. 36):

> The spider's web or network symbolised craft, cunning, and deceit. What animal, other than the human creature, was known to construct such premeditated snares for the unwary? The metaphor of the spider's snare was, however, much more than a flimsy tissue of silken cobwebs; instead ... the net or web became associated with a snare of words spun from nothing more than the malevolent interior of the gossip or calumniator.

This Arachnean deceit is memorably conveyed in Dante's description of Geryon, symbol of fraud (*Inferno* 17):

> Two paws it had, hairy unto the armpits;
> The back, and breast, and both the sides it had
> Depicted o'er with nooses and with shields,
>
> With colours more, groundwork or broidery,
> Never in cloth did Tartars make or Turks,
> Nor were such tissues by Arachne laid

There is a hint of beauty behind the grotesque, a clue that Dante himself is not immune to fraud. And if we look at the end of the previous canto, when the arrival of Geryon is described, we can see that Dante is also, in a sense, implicated in the fraud which Geryon represents. Dante acknowledges that it is hard to convince his readers that this beast is real (*Inferno* 16):

4. Arachne

> Aye, to that truth which has the face of falsehood,
> A man should close his lips as far as may be,
> Because without his fault it causes shame;
>
> But here I cannot; and, Reader, by the notes
> Of this my Comedy to thee I swear,
> So may they not be void of lasting favour,
>
> Athwart that dense and darksome atmosphere
> I saw a figure swimming upward come,
> Marvellous unto every steadfast heart.

Pamela Royston Macfie notes that an important distinction may be drawn between fraud which lurks beneath an alluring exterior – Geryon – and truth which is so fantastic it seems like a lie – Dante's description of Geryon. His poem 'may authenticate the miraculous creation of God, in spite of its own fictive status' (pp. 155-7). But ultimately, no matter how skilful a weaver of words the poet may be, the poem *is* a fiction and thus – by the high standards of literal truthfulness which the narrator himself insists on in the above quotation – at least a partial fraud. Dante's uneasy identification with Geryon replays the resemblance between Arachne and the deceitful, rapacious gods she so despises.

Edmund Spenser, in *The Faerie Queene*, can also be outed as a secret Arachnophile. At the end of his description of the Bower of Bliss, an enticing pleasure garden, Spenser introduces its mistress, the alluring but sinful enchantress Acrasia, as she dallies with her latest lover (2.12.77):

> And was arayd, or rather disarrayed,
> All in a vele of silke and silver thin,
> That hid no wit her alabaster skin,
> But rather shewed more white, if more might bee:

Ovid

> More subtile web Arachne cannot spin,
> Nor the fine nets, which oft we woven see
> Of scorched deaw, do not in th'aire more lightly flee.

This description of the web, or net, so tantalisingly flimsy, is echoed a few stanzas later when Acrasia is captured by priggish Sir Guyon and his trusty sidekick, the Palmer (2.12.81):

> The noble Elfe, and carefull Palmer drew
> So nigh them, minding nought, but lustfull game,
> That suddein forth they on them rusht, and threw
> A subtile net, which onely for the same
> The skillfull Palmer formally did frame.

The reader is invited to invoke the story of Venus and Mars, caught in Vulcan's net, and may overlook the similarities between the web which captured Acrasia and the earlier web with which she trapped her male prey. Once noted, we might go on to consider whether these two webs similarly fail in their ostensive purpose. The first one, as a garment, ought to conceal her charms but actually sets them off to greater effect. The second is meant to trap Acrasia, but the reader may not immediately be sure who has captured whom. The two pairs – the enchantress and her lover Verdant, Guyon and the Palmer – are not securely differentiated. Logically we may assume that it is the lovers who are preoccupied by 'lustfull game', but the syntax is ambiguous, and the possibility is raised that the virtuous spies are themselves not immune from lust.

'Only for the same' is a little oblique. Although A.C. Hamilton is surely correct in offering the explanation 'i.e. for the same purpose' it is significant that it needs to be explained at all. There is a similar sense of exclusion and specificity in this

4. Arachne

phrase as there is in 'nought but lustful game'; moreover the rhyme between 'game' and 'same' increases the possibility of a chime between them in the reader's mind, and thus implies that the net is associated with some lustful purpose. Another reading, tenable until the last line quoted above, might identify the rushing pair, not with Guyon and the Palmer, but with the lustful lovers; the virtuous hunters are thus the captives not the captors. We may be more inclined to such a reading because Spenser has already associated Acrasia with the use of a subtle web to (metaphorically) ensnare her victims.

But ultimately anything other than a firm separation between the web of Acrasia's garment and the Palmer's net becomes a misreading. Guyon's victory over lust is unequivocally complete (83):

> But all those pleasant bowres and Pallace brave,
> Guyon broke downe, with rigour pittilesse;
> Ne ought their goodly workmanship might save
> Them from the tempest of his wrathfulnesse ...

The Palmer's net may be unambiguous in function, but another woven surface – the text – has proved as ready to deceive and as enticing as Acrasia's own 'subtile web'. Like Dante, like Arachne herself, Spenser betrays the affinities between his own art and that of his supposed villains. His poetic tapestry seems intended to serve virtue, but the *Faerie Queene* would be a less memorable poem if sin were not sometimes allowed to escape through the net.

Ovid's tale of Arachne is firmly embedded within a network of female artists and connoisseurs. Minerva narrates the story to the Muses, who have just told her how they beat their rivals, the Pierides, in a rather similar storytelling contest. Minerva and

Ovid

Arachne are both female, and so is their audience of nymphs. This textual community of artistic women is an important part of the story's reception. Male writers – whether friendly or hostile – tend to ignore Arachne's sex, but many female responses to the tale comment on the traditional association between women and weaving or embroidery. An assertive account of this link is given by the eighteenth-century poet Anne Finch in 'A Description of One of the Pieces of Tapistry at Long-Leat, made after the famous Cartons of Raphael', which I quote at the opening of this chapter. Finch does not simply wish to revitalise this undervalued and neglected female accomplishment. Although she implies that weaving should be regarded as equal to writing, she slides from a discussion of a traditional and allowed female skill to the more masculine province of poetry:

> So much, All Arts are by the Men engross'd,
> And Our few Talents unimprov'd or cross'd;
> Even I, who on this Subject wou'd compose,
> Which the fam'd Urbin for his Pencil chose,
> (And here, in tinctur'd Wool we now behold
> Correctly follow'd in each Shade, and Fold)
> Shou'd prudently from the Attempt withdraw,
> But Inclination proves the stronger Law:
> And tho' the Censures of the World pursue
> These hardy Flights, whilst his Designs I view;
> My burden'd Thoughts, which labour for a Vent,
> Urge me t'explain in Verse, what by each Face is meant.

So although Finch seems to champion weaving, her own choice to express herself in a poem rather than a tapestry might betray a suspicion that textiles are just a little too 'feminine' to be truly

4. Arachne

great art. This tension in her position, comparable with that experienced by women about other specialisms of their sex, including motherhood, is rearticulated in a very recent response to Arachne, A.S. Byatt's meditation on the myth in the anthology *Ovid Metamorphosed*. She describes her childhood dislike of needlework, which she ascribes to her perception of it as a woman's art, and she recalls the resentment she felt when her headmistress told the school that she had written books and made tablecloths and thought the latter were the greater achievement. But eventually Byatt becomes reconciled to the 'female arts' and respects the memory of her great-aunt Thirza who was a skilled embroiderer.

Although both contestants are female it is with Arachne that female writers seem to have identified most feelingly. Indeed Minerva can become associated with male authority, as in a poem by Sara Coleridge in which she thanks Coleridge for the gift of a thimble; here she implicitly compares her husband with Minerva and herself with Arachne. Although Sara Coleridge imagines that such a splendid thimble must have been used by Minerva, allowing her to vanquish Arachne, it is the mortal weaver whose work is most vividly described, becoming (though only because its maker is crying) alive:

> And to her eyes, suffus'd with watery woe,
> Her flower-embroider'd web danc'd dim, I wist,
> Like blossom'd shrubs in a quick-moving mist:
> Till vanquish'd the despairing Maid sunk low.

The reference to the quick moving mist and the vanquished maid might just suggest a story that Arachne didn't include on her tapestry but which Ovid relates in Book 1 of the *Metamorphoses*, that of Io, who is seduced by Jupiter after he takes the form of a mist. Perhaps Sara Coleridge felt more oppressed by the brilliance of her husband than her apparently lighthearted poem would suggest. Io is later transformed into a cow and loses the power of speech. Sara Coleridge, rather less dramatically, is also muted. She confirms the connections between her husband's art and Minerva's in order to elevate his work at the expense of her own. Yet both her own feeling evocation of Arachne, and Ovid's original possible preference for the mortal weaver, undercut her expressions of modesty:

> O Bard! whom sure no common Muse inspires,
> I heard your Verse that glows with vestal fires!
> And I from unwatch'd needle's erring point
> Had surely suffer'd on each finger-joint
> Those wounds, which erst did poor Arachne meet;
> While he, the much-lov'd Object of my choice
> (My bosom thrilling with enthusiast heat),
> Pour'd on mine ear with deep impressive voice ...
> What wounds your thought-bewildering Muse might cause
> Tis well your finger-shielding gifts prevent.

Sara Coleridge's reinvention of Minerva as an oppressive figure of male authority reflects earlier traditions surrounding the goddess. The medieval moralising tradition associated her with Christ – Arachne was said to represent hypocrisy. And at the end of Aeschylus' *Oresteia* the emergence of Athena (Minerva) from the head of Zeus rather than a womb is adduced as proof that the mother is only a kind of animated incubator, not a true parent in the same way the father is. This evidence is used to pardon Orestes for killing his mother Clytemnestra.

A motherless female fulfils a similarly equivocal role in the

4. Arachne

story of an artist who understood (unlike Arachne) that goddesses prefer to be worshipped rather than challenged, the sculptor Pygmalion.

5

Pygmalion

Paulina: Music; awake her; strike!
   Music
   (To Hermione) 'Tis time. Descend. Be stone no more.
Approach.
Strike all that look upon with marvel. Come,
I'll fill your grave up. Stir. Nay, come away.
Bequeath to death your numbness, for from him
Dear life redeems you.
   (To Leontes) You perceive she stirs.
   Hermione slowly descends
Start not. Her actions shall be holy as
You hear my spell is lawful.
                    Shakespeare, *The Winter's Tale*

I started from my sleep with horror; a cold dew covered my forehead, my teeth chattered, and every limb became convulsed: when, by the dim and yellow light of the moon, as it forced its way through the window shutters, I beheld the wretch – the miserable monster whom I had created. He held up the curtain of the bed; and his eyes, if eyes they may be called, were fixed on me. His jaws opened, and he muttered some inarticulate sounds, while a grin wrinkled his cheeks. He might have spoken, but I did not hear; one hand was stretched out, seemingly to detain me, but I escaped, and rushed down stairs. I took refuge in the courtyard belonging to the house which I inhabited; where I remained during the rest of the night, walking up and down in the greatest agitation, listening attentively, catching and fearing each sound as if it were to announce the approach of the demoniacal corpse to which I had so miserably given life.

Mary Shelley, *Frankenstein*

In the 2003 war on Iraq one of the most memorable images, reproduced again and again by television and newspapers, was the statue of Saddam Hussein being toppled by Iraqi civilians and US troops in apparent celebration of the downfall of his regime. This act of violence simultaneously reflected a new political and military reality and enacted a symbolic revenge on the body of Saddam himself.

The symbolic power of statues which represent leaders and celebrities, their capacity to become semi-animated in our imaginations as projections of the original, is comparatively easy to understand. But it would seem that this power is not confined to lifelike representations of well known figures; the idea of the statue more generally has a similar hold over our imagination. Even a statue which does not represent any known person seems somehow imbued with the potential for life. Sigmund Freud (drawing on the work of his contemporary Ernst Jentsch) identifies the waxwork doll or automaton, lifeless but unmistakably lifelike, as the clearest manifestation of the 'uncanny'. This way of looking at dolls did not originate with Jentsch. Fanny Kemble's lurid account of her distaste for dolls, included in the actress' 1878 *Record of a Girlhood*, captures their sinister quality perfectly:

> They always affected me with a grim sense of being a mockery of the humanity they were supposed to represent; there was something uncanny, not to say ghastly, in the doll existence and its mimicry of babyhood to me, and I had a nervous

5. Pygmalion

dislike, not unmixed with fear, of the smiling simulacra that girls are all supposed to love with a species of prophetic maternal instinct.

The doll's potential to disturb has been exploited by many writers and artists, most notoriously in the *Child's Play* films. Another memorable example from popular culture is the animation of the autons in the 1970 *Doctor Who* adventure, *Spearhead from Space*. The autons appear to be no more than shop window dummies, but when triggered remotely by the evil Nestene consciousness they spring to murderous life. Their hairless heads and sightless eyes lend them a compellingly sinister blank neutrality.

On first reading, Ovid's story of Pygmalion could scarcely contrast more strongly with that of the truly 'uncanny' autons. A sculptor creates a perfect woman out of ivory. Entranced by its beauty he dresses it with clothes and jewels as though it were a real woman and eventually prays to Venus for a wife just like her. The goddess grants his wish by animating the statue herself, who becomes Pygmalion's bride. Although it seems that Venus is the power behind the miracle, Ovid's poetry suggests that the sculptor's marvellous artistry is the true agent of metamorphosis (10.283-6):

> As he touched the ivory it grew softer and lost its former obduracy; it dimpled and yielded beneath his fingers just as Hymettian wax, when it melts in the sun, can be worked by the thumb into many forms, becoming pliable through handling.

Clearly it is possible to see this as a strongly affirmative story. An apparently impossible dream becomes a reality thanks to the combined power of love and art. There is generally a kind of inbuilt bias in favour of any kind of artist in the *Metamorphoses*, a sense of fellow feeling with creators such as Arachne and Mulciber, and we may assume that Ovid sympathised with Pygmalion's pursuit of beauty and love. The bond between poetry and sculpture is particularly in evidence in the myth's reception, where it is frequently manipulated to playful effect. George Marston, in his erotic 'The Metamorphosis of Pygmalion's Image' (1598), tricksily elides the sculptor's art with the poet's when, in his blazon of the statue's charms, he tells us that 'her breasts like polished ivory appear'. Of course her breasts *are* ivory – but poets, like sculptors, enjoy manufacturing women out of jewels and other precious substances, a habit which Shakespeare parodies in Sonnet 130:

> My mistress' eyes are nothing like the sun;
> Coral is far more red than her lips' red;
> If snow be white, why then her breasts are dun;
> If hairs be wires, black wires grow on her head.

One of Ovid's most recent translators, David Slavitt, plays the same kind of trick on the reader as Marston:

> One, especially lovely,
> He fashioned out of a piece of snowy ivory flesh
> Could never have duplicated.

Ivory might as easily be an adjective qualifying flesh as a noun, and only as our eye travels to the next line do we realise we have been deceived. This kind of play is only possible because so many writers have described women as though they were precious works of art rather than living beings. This objec-

5. Pygmalion

tification of women inheres in Ovid's story, and for modern, female readers in particular, the apparent bias towards a male perspective, the fact that the miracle was performed for the gratification of Pygmalion's desire rather than for Galatea's benefit, may be a source of unease. Nor are such readers necessarily reading against the grain, for there are clues within the *Metamorphoses* itself which seem to undercut the story and suggest that Ovid's point of view is by no means identical with Pygmalion's. Is there, for example, any link between the 'snowy' white statue Pygmalion carves and the similarly 'snowy' heifers which he carves up to provide a fitting sacrifice for Venus?

Like many tales within the poem, the story of Pygmalion is told by an inset narrator rather than by Ovid himself. As with Chaucer's *Canterbury Tales*, to get the full sense of each tale in the *Metamorphoses* we must pay attention to its teller. The narrator of Pygmalion is Orpheus, and he speaks to an audience of wild beasts and birds, charmed by his voice. At this point in the narrative Orpheus has already, for the second time, lost his wife Eurydice whom he had rescued from the Underworld but forfeited by looking back at her before they left the Valley of Avernus. He responded to his loss by shunning women and enjoying instead the love of beautiful boys. The character and history of Orpheus thus may be reflected in his account of the sculptor. Pygmalion similarly shuns the love of women – though because the whole sex fills him with disgust rather than because of any specific disappointment. He too seeks satisfaction in a substitute, a statue rather than a boy. And, like Orpheus, he gives a woman life – though it is ivory rather than a corpse that he animates. As he does not lose her, the story might reflect a wish-fulfilment fantasy on the part of Orpheus who is unable to retain his own revived Eurydice.

An interesting parallel from *The Canterbury Tales* is 'The

Wife of Bath's Tale'. The Wife, a much married woman past her prime, tells of a youth who is obliged to marry an ugly hag as punishment for rape, but is reprieved when she is transformed into a beautiful girl at the tale's climax. We sense that the Wife of Bath wishes for a similar miracle to give her back her beauty – and a handsome husband.

The tale of Pygmalion may also be illuminated by the very next story Orpheus narrates, the incestuous love of Myrrha for her father Cinyras. Significantly, Cinyras is the grandson of Pygmalion and the statue; the unnatural liaison between a father and his daughter may be mapped on to the story of Pygmalion's love for his creation. In this new context the sculptor's passion is more likely to seem fetishistic and perverse than idealistic or fairytale-like. Verbal links between the two tales underline the affinity between them. For example, when Pygmalion prays to Venus he doesn't dare ask for his ivory maid herself; instead, after some hesitation, he asks for one similar to her. When Cinyras asks Myrrha what kind of husband she desires she uses the same equivocation to hide her true wishes and requests 'one like you'. In other words, each conceals their real desire by claiming they only want something 'like' it. And in each case this shift makes a perverse ideal natural, a lovely woman not a lovely statue, a man like one's father, not one's father himself.

And even without looking for disturbing analogues outside the tale, we can find fuel for discomfort in Pygmalion's rejection of women. The Propoetides in particular are blamed for his misogyny. This group of women denied the divinity of Venus, and the goddess punished them by forcing them into prostitution. Such a life eventually hardened them until they turned to stone. As Genevieve Liveley points out, there is a tendency to misread this compressed little narrative and identify prostitution as their crime rather than their punishment. Liveley conjectures

5. Pygmalion

that their crime may be celibacy – certainly it must be some activity (or inactivity) which contrasts with prostitution or the punishment would have no force. To be reminded that prostitution is the punishment inflicted by the goddess rather than a crime committed against her may reinflect our sense of Venus within the narrative; her cruelty towards women whose only crime may be celibacy contrasts unpleasantly with her provision of a biddable love object for a man who avowedly 'felt repugnance for the countless faults which Nature had embedded in women's minds' (10.244-5). This is the dynamic of Margaret Atwood's *The Handmaid's Tale*, whose powerful men rob women of their freedom, forcing them into acquiescent wife/handmaid roles and compelling those who demonstrate sexual or intellectual rebellion to work in approved brothels.

The uneasy pitting of transgressive against compliant women colours much of the tale's reception. The Propoetides themselves figure in very few responses. However, many texts which allude to Pygmalion suggest, unlike Ovid, that the sculptor based his masterpiece on a living model; tension is generated between the woman and the work of art which mimics her. Often it is suggested that, because autonomy is an unattractive female trait, a painting or sculpture of a woman may triumph over the model herself. In Charles Cotton's 'The Picture' (1689) this possibility is raised but immediately discounted by the poet who is trying to persuade his mistress to let him have her portrait:

> Perchance you fear Idolatry
> Would make the Image prove
> A Woman fit for love;
> Or give it such a soul as shone
> Through fond Pigmalion's living stone,
> That so I might abandon thee.

He swears that seeing her picture would help him stay faithful to her when they are apart. Less gallant, James Robertson, in a poem published in 1773, sees definite advantages in a speechless consort:

> To please Pygmalion, Heav'n inspir'd with Life
> A Tongueless Stone, of which he made a Wife;
> Wou'd Heav'n, all-gracious, hear Asino's moan,
> His Wife – her Tongue at least – wou'd soon be Stone.

Charles Sisson's take on this play with reverse metamorphosis is particularly unpleasant. A poem which begins as a fairly literal translation of Pygmalion's tale concludes thus:

> To his surprise the girl grew warm;
> He slobbered and she slobbered back
>
> – This is that famous mutual flame.
> The worst of all was yet to come.
>
> Although he often wished her back
> In silent marble, good and cold
>
> The bitch retained her human heat,
> The conquest of a stone by art.
>
> May Venus keep me from all hope
> And let me turn my love to stone.

The disagreeable and unexpected verb 'slobbered' encourages us to import the full animalistic potential of 'bitch' into the poem. This in turn makes it difficult to avoid allowing 'heat' – warmth, life, passion – to be contaminated by the phrase 'on

5. Pygmalion

heat'. A living woman, for Sisson's Pygmalion, is a rutting animal. Stone is clearly preferable.

The Pygmalion in Henry James' short story 'The Last of the Valerii' seems to have similar preferences. The story's narrator is an American whose young goddaughter, Martha, marries an Italian count, Camillo Valerio. Their happy marriage is disrupted when the Count becomes obsessed with a statue of Juno, discovered during the course of an archaeological excavation of his grounds. The narrator anxiously charts the couple's growing estrangement, which, we are led to believe, arises from Valerio's atavistic return to the pagan beliefs of his ancestors (embodied in the Juno). But can a different interpretation of the Count's obsession be excavated from the narrative?

One of the tale's several oddnesses is the choice of a majestic clothed Juno (rather than the more obvious Venus) as the focus for the Count's obsession. It might seem that the statue's power is not, or not primarily, supposed to be erotic. In his discussion of the tale, J. Hillis Miller suggests that Juno represents a powerful mother figure 'of the sort that demands of her male children the ultimate sacrifice of their masculinity. This sacrifice is mimed in the blood sacrifice Camillo performs' (p. 231). (Martha and her godfather discover blood at the statue's feet.) He goes on to suggest that her one flaw – a broken hand – is a further symbol of castration. The precise provenance of the blood on Juno's altar remains unclear; the godfather seeks to reassure Martha: ' "Be sure it's very innocent," I said; "a lamb, a kid, or a sucking calf" ' (p. 823). We infer that he is assuring her that the Count has harmed no other human, though a hint at self-castration might certainly be present. But for Hillis Miller the Count's implied emasculation is not significant for what it suggests about his sexuality. Like most commentators he believes that the Count's struggle is between an alluring but

131

proscribed paganism (represented by Juno) and a wholesome but depressing modernity (represented by Martha and her godfather).

But further evidence in the text suggests that the unearthed statue might represent, not the buried past of the Count's race, but his suppressed homosexuality. I have already shown that, in its original Ovidian context, Pygmalion's statue fulfils the same function as young boys do for Orpheus: both are a replacement for unsatisfactory women. Because the statue in Ovid is evoked so powerfully as a heteroerotic love object the reader is unlikely to dwell on this link. But James carefully de-eroticises the statue – by transforming her into a clothed Juno – allowing other interpretive possibilities room for play. We are encouraged to reflect on the statue's identity, to see James' choice of Juno as anything but arbitrary, by the narrator's speculations before she is discovered (p. 807):

> I *may* be summoned to welcome another Antinous back to fame,
> – a Venus, a Faun, an Augustus.

The subjects which run through his mind have their own significance. We are reminded that James might have made the Count's obsession focus on the ideally sexual female, Venus. A quite different scenario is suggested by the narrator's very first conjecture: Antinous, the young lover of the Emperor Hadrian, whose reputed beauty made him a favourite subject for sculptors. The narrator's initial choice of a homoerotic focus of desire, the youth Antinous, perhaps gives us a clue how to decode a curious dual perspective in the way the story is told. A strange faultline runs through the godfather's narrative, making it difficult for the reader to piece together the whole story – and, particularly, to reconstitute the narrator's original impressions.

5. Pygmalion

In hindsight, as he writes, he knows perfectly well that the Juno is responsible for the Count's alienation from Martha. The entire tale is narrated from this perspective – from its first discovery we are aware of the Juno as a portentous and rather threatening figure. However initially, at the time when the events actually took place, the godfather was in the dark as to the cause of the Count's strange behaviour. Yet because we always have the benefit of the narrator's hindsight, we don't immediately realise that he hasn't guessed that paganism is at the root of his goddaughter's marriage problems. In fact it is only after rereading the story that the potential significance and possible nature of the narrator's interim suspicions are made clear. The godfather's uneasy sense that Martha 'was the least bit strangely mated' and his description of her puzzlement at Camillo's estrangement from her, for example, reflect impressions that predate his discovery of the Juno's impact on the Count (p. 813):

> She sat at times with her eyes fixed on him with a kind of imploring curiosity, as if pitying surprise held resentment yet awhile in check. What passed between them in private, I had, of course, no warrant to inquire. Nothing, I imagined, – and that was the misery! ... From his wife he kept his face inexorably averted; and when she approached him with some persuasive caress, he received it with an ill-concealed shudder.

An important clue to what might have gone through the narrator's mind at this point can be found in his description of the Count's fascination with another statue, that of Hermes, which had always stood in his grounds. The godfather finds the Count sitting in his garden at night gazing at it. For the reader the statue is most likely to figure paganism and act as a surrogate for the Juno. But it is possible that the godfather reads the signals quite differently. The Count's description of the Hermes suggests a figure both effeminate and sensual 'pouting his great lips'; he explains that he used to think the statue frightening but finds that now it 'suggests the most delightful images' (p. 815).

> The Hermes, for a wonder, had kept his nose; and when I reflected that my dear Countess was being neglected for this senseless pagan block, I secretly promised myself to come the next day with a hammer and deal him such a lusty blow as would make him too ridiculous for a sentimental tête-à-tête.

This reflection seems rather jocular and inconsequential and the reader may skim over its surface implication – that the Hermes is in some way a sexual rival to the Countess. Because the Juno is so portentously and mysteriously potent within the story it is easy to overlook the way the Hermes apparently affects the narrator. But if we remember that the godfather does not yet realise the impact the Juno has had on the Count, his reaction to the Hermes incident provides us with a further clue that homosexuality is suspected (p. 815):

> Meanwhile, however, the Count's infatuation was no laughing matter, and I expressed my sincerest conviction when I said, after a pause, that I should recommend him to see either a priest or a physician.

We, the readers, have been fully primed about the Juno's significance and (oddly) have been misled by the narrator into thinking that he too, at this time, saw matters the way he has encouraged us to see them. Thus we will probably assume that the godfather's feelings of disgust mixed with pity, and his

5. Pygmalion

advice that the Count consult either a priest or a doctor, are prompted by fears that he is becoming a pagan. Yet the narrator's assumption that medicine and the church hold the answers also makes sense within a concealed (but far more probable) context of latent homosexuality – a context we would be more likely to identify if we had not had the wool of 'paganism' pulled so tightly over our eyes. The narrator surely misleads us, for it is only *after* this exchange that the godfather as character (as opposed to the godfather as narrator who has known it all along) learns that it is Paganism that has won Camillo away from his bride. Before this his anxieties are expressed in a way which makes far more sense within a context of sexual impropriety: 'How should I treat him, what stand should I take, what course did Martha's happiness and dignity demand?' (p. 815). When the Count finally articulates his pagan impulses, the godfather's first reaction is one of amused relief (pp. 817-18):

> I seemed to touch the source of his trouble, and my relief was great, for my discovery made me feel like bursting into laughter .... In my gratitude, I was able to thank any gods he pleased .... A sturdy young Latin I had called Camillo; sturdier, indeed, than I had dreamed him! Discretion was now misplaced ....

Although anxiety about Martha's 'dignity' might easily be ascribed to suspicion that the Count was having an affair with a woman, the emphasis on his 'sturdiness' (rather than say his 'worthiness') perhaps implies a pleased relief at discovering that he is after all thoroughly masculine. Finally Martha solves the problem by ordering that the Juno be reburied in the earth, leaving the Count apparently cured though he still secretly possesses her beautiful marble hand, which had broken off when she was first excavated.

Martha's victory is unusual. In other responses to the Pygmalion story woman and art object are plotted more violently against one another – with the latter generally winning the fight. Three of the most striking examples of this motif – a poem, a short story and a film – are all products of the American Gothic tradition. Washington Allston's poem 'The Paint King' (1813) tells the horrific tale of Ellen, who falls in love with a picture of Pygmalion only for the artist to come to life and grind her up to make the paints with which he will create the portrait of his own love, the fair Geraldine:

> Then Ellen, all reeking, he laid;
> With a rock for his muller he crush'd every bone,
> But, though ground to jelly, still, still did she groan;
> For life had forsook not the maid.
>
> Now reaching his palette, with masterly care
> Each tint on its surface he spread;
> The blue of her eyes, and the brown of her hair,
> And the pearl and the white of her forehead so fair,
> And her lips' and her cheeks' rosy red.

However his project ultimately fails because he lacks any black pigment – a mouse has run off with the unfortunate Ellen's pupils.

A strikingly 'uncanny' variation on the portrait as love rival theme is described in Edgar Allen Poe's 'The Oval Portrait' (1850). In this short story a young artist becomes so absorbed in the portrait he is painting of his wife that he fails to realise that she is dying. The impression is created that the picture sucks the life from its model, and its status as an actively malevolent rival is hinted at when we are told that the girl should not

5. Pygmalion

have married the painter because he 'already [had] a bride in his Art'. The tale's climax describes the portrait's completion:

> ... for one moment, the painter stood entranced before the work which he had wrought; but in the next, while he yet gazed, he grew tremulous and very pallid, and aghast, and crying with a loud voice, 'This is indeed *Life* itself!' turned suddenly to regard his beloved: – *She was dead!*

The enmity between woman and replica is most evident in Bryan Forbes' 1975 film version of Ira Levin's novel *The Stepford Wives*. The film's heroine Joanna, played by Katharine Ross, is appalled to find that the women in her new home town have no interests outside the home and are completely submissive to their husbands. Her suspicions are aroused when her feisty best friend is transformed overnight into a domestic goddess. Joanna begins to investigate the town's mysterious Men's Association which holds secret meetings from which all women are excluded. Eventually she realises that the club is creating perfect automata with which the real women are replaced, and is finally strangled by her own replicant. In this film the idle fantasies of writers such as James Robertson have become reality, although the fact that the female robot, not the men, destroys Joanna points to a subtler message about women's own possible complicity in their subjugation.

Although its exploration of the Pygmalion motif is less obviously misogynistic, Alfred Hitchcock's *Vertigo* offers a more subtly sinister account of a man's obsession with shaping a woman to conform to his desires. The film's hero, Scottie, witnessed what appeared to be the tragic accidental death of his mysterious love, Madeleine (played by Kim Novak), when she fell from a bell tower. Haunted by her loss, Scottie starts thinking that every blonde woman wearing grey he glimpses may be Madeleine, but is one day struck by a girl who is nothing like her – a brunette called Judy. He courts her and gradually persuades her to 'become' Madeleine, changing her hair colour, clothes and make up. Meanwhile the viewer has learnt that the resemblance is not an illusion – Judy acted the part of 'Madeleine' as part of a plot allowing the real Madeleine's husband to murder her.

Although Scottie is an essentially likeable character – he is played by perennial 'nice guy' James Stewart – we become increasingly uneasy about his pursuit of Madeleine and sympathise with Judy when she expresses resentment at being changed into a very different woman. Whereas Madeleine was remote, even glacial, Judy is sassy and sceptical. While Ovid's Pygmalion seems to sculpt his statue into life after praying to Venus, Scottie appears to be using cosmetic arts to turn a real woman into a fake one. It is as though Pygmalion were trying to turn his wife back into a statue. However the cinematic context complicates our urge to distinguish 'real' Judy from 'false' Madeleine. Both roles are, we may assume, equally artificial.

In this film, as in so many responses to the myth, there is a link between the internal Pygmalion (here Scottie) and the author (here Hitchcock). Scottie's urge to turn Judy into a blonde goddess reflects Hitchcock's fascination with manufactured blonde heroines, played by Grace Kelly, Eve Marie Saint and Kim Novak herself. The movement from 'reality' to 'art' enacted by Scottie/Hitchcock is reflected in the heroine's disturbing double death, a reversal of the myth's climax of animation. Madeleine's first death was a feint. But having painstakingly recreated his beloved on a canvas of flesh and blood Scottie learns of the conspiracy and takes her to the scene of the crime as a punishment. She is terrified and jumps from the bell tower in earnest.

5. Pygmalion

Like Orpheus – and it is interesting to see this myth paired yet again with that of Pygmalion – Scottie has lost his love for the second time. It is as though the transformation of Judy into Madeleine, a beautiful automaton, was not enough, and, having turned her back into a statue, Scottie has to destroy her as well.

Although, as we have seen, there are sinister, unnatural undercurrents already present in Ovid's version of the tale, one text in particular is probably responsible for the frequent darkening of the story over the course of its nineteenth- and twentieth-century reception. Mary Shelley's *Frankenstein* (1818) is not an obvious descendant of Pygmalion, yet the novel's interrogation of humanity's parameters and powerful presentation of animation exerted a significant influence on many later treatments of the myth. The monster repels us but also forces us to question our own prejudices; as we watch him being rebuffed by humanity we are bound to reflect on the ethical dilemmas involved in the creation of artificial life. Frankenstein is overwhelmed by his creation when the monster seeks to destroy everything he holds dear, and almost coerces his maker into giving him a mate. This theme of a creature gaining uncanny control over its maker is curiously echoed in Shelley's 1831 introduction to her novel. The description of its genesis casts her as Pygmalion, the text as Galatea, demanding to be sculpted into life:

> When I placed my head on my pillow, I did not sleep, nor could I be said to think. My imagination, unbidden, possessed and guided me, gifting the successive images that arose in my mind with a vividness far beyond the usual bounds of a reverie. *I saw with shut eyes, but acute mental vision,* – I saw the pale student of unhallowed arts kneeling beside the thing he had put together.

This evocation of a nightmarish dream state as the prelude to creation is paralleled in Ted Hughes' sinister adaptation of Ovid's tale:

> Yet he still dreamed of woman.
> He dreamed
> Unbrokenly awake as asleep
> The perfect body of a perfect woman –
> Though this dream
> Was not so much the dream of a perfect woman
> As a spectre, sick of unbeing,
> That had taken possession of his body
> To find herself a life.

Both Shelley and Hughes disturb our intuitive sense that the creator takes precedence over what he creates, skewing the original tale's dynamic of power. Similar ambiguities are generated by Ridley Scott's 1982 film, *Blade Runner*.

Both Ovid's version of the Pygmalion story and *Frankenstein* feature climactic scenes in which an inanimate being is miraculously brought to life. There is no such epiphany in *Blade Runner*. The existence of the 'replicants', perfect replicas of humanity, is a given of the film, and its aim, and that of its hero, is to destroy or 'retire' these troubling simulacra whose capacity to develop emotions is perceived as a threat to humankind. Death not life is the goal of its anti-Pygmalion, Deckard. The executions he carries out are presented at some length, and the film's insistent emphasis on the replicants' physiology, in particular their capacity to bleed, makes them seem human at the point of death.

Some of *Blade Runner*'s most striking moments of tension are provided when a test is administered to subjects whose humanity is in doubt. The aim of the test is to measure

5. Pygmalion

emotional reactions via objective criteria such as pupil dilation and heartbeat, and thus distinguish between robot and human. The effectiveness of this test is put under strain by the film's most perfect replicant, the beautiful Rachael, an experimental model who has been implanted with false memories, making her believe herself to be 'real'. The tension generated by each administration of the test reflects a more pervasive anxiety surrounding the increasing difficulty experienced when policing the boundaries between animate and inanimate life. In many ways the replicants seem more human than the humans themselves – they are resourceful, passionate and fiercely loyal to one another. Their leader, Roy, saves the life of his pursuer, Deckard, when he has the chance to let him fall to his death, and speaks with moving intensity of his adventurous life, which he knows is about to come to an end. For replicants are programmed to terminate after just four years, to prevent them developing and learning beyond a safely contained level. This poignantly brief life span encourages the viewer to see them as hyper-human rather than humanity's antithesis.

Blade Runner interiorises the powerful Pygmalion myth, forcing its hero to question his own ontological status. As is so often the case in responses to this story, the film's status as a fictional construct has a part to play in its development of the myth. As a character in a screenplay Deckard, like Rachael and the other replicants, has no real past although subjectively he is aware of family memories, signalled by the photos he hoards. The same could of course be said of any fictional character, but this film explicitly encourages us to reflect on Deckard's problematically sketchy previous life. A mysterious shot of a unicorn – a childhood fantasy perhaps – gains significance when Deckard's sinister colleague, an Origami enthusiast, leaves a tiny model of a unicorn by his door at the end of the film. We have already seen Deckard break the news to Rachael that he can 'read' her mind because he knows which memories have been implanted in her brain. But perhaps Deckard is similarly vulnerable. It would seem possible that he, like Rachael, is only a replicant – this would explain his special ability to track his fellows down – and that his 'memory' of a unicorn is known to those around him because they are his creators. Yet, in keeping with the film's complex presentation of simulated life, the image of the unicorn has a further significance. As an unactualised possibility – a fantasy like the story of Pygmalion itself – the unicorn symbolises the quintessentially human power of imagination. The image which signals Deckard's possible replicancy also in a strange way proves his fundamental humanity.

6

Ovid in the Third Millennium

The very last lines of the *Metamorphoses* anticipate Ovid's poetic immortality (15.877-9):

> Wherever Rome's might extends itself over conquered lands, my name shall be on the lips of the people and, if the prophesies of poets have any truth, my fame will live forever.

We are conditioned to be sceptical of such hubristic pronouncements, and tend to assume that ambitious over-reachers will eventually be punished. Such is the fate of Shelley's imaginary tyrant Ozymandias, whose former glory is now all but forgotten, his colossal statue reduced to a few scattered fragments:

> And on the pedestal these words appear:
> 'My name is Ozymandias, king of kings:
> Look on my works, ye Mighty, and despair!'
> Nothing beside remains. Round the decay
> Of that colossal wreck, boundless and bare
> The lone and level sands stretch far away.

Yet Ovid's bold prophecy has (so far) been triumphantly fulfilled. A major factor in his success, as I hope this book has already demonstrated, is the flexible variety of the *Metamorphoses*, and its amenability to a range of readings. Although the poem has been consistently influential, each generation of readers has been drawn to it for different reasons, and singled out different stories for special praise. Each age finds (or contrives) something peculiarly relevant to its own preoccupations in the *Metamorphoses*; Ovid resembles the timeless musician on Keats' Grecian Urn: 'happy melodist, unwearied,/ For ever piping songs for ever new'.

It is initially easy to agree with Michael Hofmann and James Lasdun when, in their introduction to *After Ovid*, they characterise Ovid as a peculiarly 'modern' poet:

> Then, too, the stories have direct, obvious and powerful affinities with contemporary reality. They offer a mythical key to most of the more extreme forms of human behaviour and suffering, especially ones we think of as peculiarly modern ....

But is there really something about our own historical moment which makes today's readers uniquely responsive to Ovid? Or is it not possible that Chaucer, Shakespeare and the rest similarly found something 'modern' in Ovid, even if they did not articulate this perception as explicitly as Hofmann and Lasdun? Borrowing Stravinsky's praise of Beethoven's *Grosse Fuge*, might we not say that the *Metamorphoses* is 'an absolutely contemporary work which will be contemporary forever'?

If each age finds itself mirrored in the *Metamorphoses*, what will tomorrow's readers find most compelling about Ovid's masterpiece? Up to a point it is easy to anticipate how the development of certain technologies, for example, might make us look at some of his stories in a new light. Research into human cloning and artificial intelligence has perhaps not yet impinged on our daily life, but these and other discoveries have become part of the furniture of our minds and therefore part of the way we respond to Ovidian tales such as Pygmalion. The human

6. Ovid in the Third Millennium

imagination anticipates and to some extent predetermines scientific advances – one must be able to conceptualise a robot before one attempts to create one – and one of the earliest such conceptualisations, it might be argued, is Pygmalion's statue herself. There are of course differences between Pygmalion's Galatea and Ridley Scott's replicants. The tale of Pygmalion – together with other Ovidian marvels such as the near extinction of the human race following the flood – now makes us reflect on the power of mankind rather than the power of the gods.

But these are shifts in emphasis not of substance. Will the *Metamorphoses* be read and interpreted in ways as yet unimaginable? This book has shown how Ovid can be used as a touchstone to gauge the different preoccupations and biases of successive generations. But if, as the testimony of the past two thousand years would seem to suggest, Ovid is indeed for all time, then the future as well as the past is embedded in the *Metamorphoses*. The discoveries and cultural shifts of tomorrow may turn readers to quite different stories in the poem from those I have discussed in this book, ones which are now largely overlooked. Boreas' wooing of Orithyia perhaps, or the tale of Ocyrhoë the prophetess, who mysteriously metamorphoses into a mare. Whether later generations do indeed find new meaning in hitherto neglected episodes or discover instead a fresh significance in consistently influential tales such as those of Pygmalion and Narcissus, it seems likely that Ovid will continue to inspire readers and writers far into the future.

> When old age shall this generation waste,
> Thou shalt remain, in midst of other woe
> Than ours, a friend to man ....
> Keats, 'Ode on a Grecian Urn'

Note on Translations

Readers with some Latin will find the Loeb edition useful. This has an English prose translation (by Frank Justus Miller) facing the Latin text. Other readers have many good – though very different – poetic translations from which to choose.

The earliest important translation is that of Arthur Golding (1567). This was used by Shakespeare and, although generally pretty faithful to Ovid, is a very 'English' translation – it is written in fourteeners and makes use of many colloquial words and expressions. Golding's Ovid has recently been reissued by Penguin. George Sandys' 1626 translation into iambic pentameter is an important work, and includes an interesting commentary on the stories. But poetically it is easily eclipsed by the version of 1717, edited by Sir Samuel Garth and translated by a number of different poets, including Dryden, Gay and Addison. The rhyming couplets capture Ovid's pointed wit, and even the lesser known contributors generally do full justice to the poem. Garth's *Metamorphoses* has recently been republished by Wordsworth Classics, and I would strongly recommend it.

But those who prefer a modern translation of the *Metamorphoses* are also well served. The best known complete translation is probably A.D. Melville's 1986 version. This is a faithful, careful rendering into blank verse, and is widely used by students. Some (including me) may prefer David Slavitt's more quirky translation, published in 1994. This includes odd little modernisations and interjections which are true to the spirit, if not the letter, of the original.

Many readers will first become acquainted with the *Metamorphoses* through Ted Hughes' much praised *Tales from Ovid*, free translations of the principal stories. Also noteworthy is

Ovid

Hofmann and Lasdun's *After Ovid*, an anthology of responses to the *Metamorphoses* by a number of well known poets including Carol Ann Duffy, Seamus Heaney and Derek Mahon. But very few of these contributions could be classed as translations – they are nearly all freely inventive adaptations.

Full bibliographical details of all these translations may be found in the bibliography.

Further Reading

This is an extremely selective list. For further ideas consult the much more extensive bibliographies included in many of the books detailed below. Full bibliographical details of my own recommendations are given in the bibliography.

A great deal has been written on the *Metamorphoses*, particularly over the last twenty years. L.P. Wilkinson's *Ovid Recalled* is a classic early study which heralded the late twentieth-century revival of interest in Ovid's works. Sara Mack's *Ovid* deals with the poet's complete oeuvre and is a lively, readable introduction aimed at undergraduates. For those who want a slightly more advanced, though still accessible, account of the *Metamorphoses*, I recommend Joseph B. Solodow's *The World of Ovid's Metamorphoses*. The recent *Cambridge Companion to Ovid* is another very useful volume; it contains several essays on the *Metamorphoses*. Its editor, Philip Hardie, has recently published *Ovid's Poetics of Illusion*, which I recommend to anyone who is interested in reading Ovid in the light of recent developments in criticism and literary theory.

Readers who wish to find out more about Ovid's reception in English literature might begin by looking at *Ovid Renewed*, an excellent collection of essays edited by Charles Martindale. Other useful volumes include Leonard Barkan's impressive and readable account of Ovid's impact on Renaissance culture, *The Gods Made Flesh*, and my own *The Metamorphosis of Ovid: From Chaucer to Ted Hughes*. Another particularly welcome addition to this topic, although it is not specifically about Ovid, is Geoffrey Miles' *Classical Mythology in English Literature*, an introductory account of Greek myth which also includes mini anthologies of poems about Orpheus, Venus and Adonis, and Pygmalion. Studies have been written of several individual writers' debt to Ovid; of most interest to the general reader is Jonathan Bate's acclaimed *Shakespeare and Ovid*.

Readers may wish to find out more about the individual myths discussed in this book. There are several studies of the Pygmalion legend to choose from. Kenneth Gross's *The Dream of the Moving Statue* and J. Hillis Miller's *Versions of Pygmalion* are both challenging and suggestive, while Essaka Joshua's recent *Pygmalion and Galatea* is a more straightforward history of the myth's reception in English literature. Mary E. Barnard's *The Myth of Apollo and Daphne from Ovid to Quevedo* and John Heath's *Actaeon, the Unmannerly Intruder: The Myth and its Meaning in Classical Literature*, although rather more specialised, contain much interesting material. For those who want to find out more about Philomela and Arachne a good starting point would be Patricia Klindienst Joplin's influential article 'The Voice of the Shuttle is Ours'. (This is available on the internet as an electronic text.) Finally, I recommend a book which discusses the phenomenon of metamorphosis more widely, Marina Warner's *Fantastic Metamorphoses, Other Worlds*.

Works Cited and Consulted

Barkan, Leonard, *The Gods Made Flesh: Metamorphosis and the Pursuit of Paganism* (New Haven & London: Yale University Press 1986).

Barnard, Mary E., *The Myth of Apollo and Daphne from Ovid to Quevedo: Love, Agon and the Grotesque* (Durham: Duke University Press 1987).

Bate, Jonathan, *Shakespeare and Ovid* (Oxford: Clarendon Press 1993).

Boehrer, Bruce Thomas, 'Bestial Buggery in *A Midsummer Night's Dream*', in *The Production of English Renaissance Culture*, edited by David Lee Miller, Sharon O'Dair and Harold Weber (Ithaca NY: Cornell University Press 1994), pp. 125-30.

Brown, Sarah Annes, *The Metamorphosis of Ovid: From Chaucer to Ted Hughes* (London: Duckworth 1999).

Brown, Sarah Annes, *Devoted Sisters: Representations of the Sister Relationship in Nineteenth-Century British and American Literature* (Aldershot: Ashgate 2003).

Dante Alighieri, *The Inferno*, translated by Henry Wadsworth Longfellow (London: Routledge 1867).

Euripides, *Three Tragedies*, edited by David Grene and Richmond Lattimore (Chicago & London: University of Chicago Press 1968).

Garth, Sir Samuel, ed., *Ovid's Metamorphoses* (1717) edited by Garth Tissol (Ware: Wordsworth 1998).

Golding, Arthur, *Ovid's Metamorphoses* (1567) edited by Madeleine Forey (London: Penguin 2002).

Gross, Kenneth, *The Dream of the Moving Statue* (Ithaca NY & London: Cornell University Press 1992).

Ovid

Hardie, Philip, Barchiesi, Alessandro and Hinds, Stephen, *Ovidian Transformations: Essays on Ovid's Metamorphoses and its Reception* (Cambridge: Cambridge Philological Society 1999).
Hardie, Philip, *Ovid's Poetics of Illusion* (Cambridge: Cambridge University Press 2002).
Hardie, Philip, ed., *The Cambridge Companion to Ovid* (Cambridge: Cambridge University Press 2002).
Heath, John, *Actaeon, the Unmannerly Intruder: The Myth and its Meaning in Classical Literature* (New York: P. Lang 1992).
Héritier, Françoise, *Two Sisters and their Mother: The Anthropology of Incest* (New York & London: Zone 1999).
Hofmann, Michael, and Lasdun, James, *After Ovid* (London, Faber & Faber 1994).
Hopkins, David, ed., *Ovid* (London: Everyman 1998).
Hughes, Ted, *Tales from Ovid* (London: Faber & Faber 1997).
James, Henry, *Complete Stories*, 5 vols (New York: Literary Classics of the United States 1999), vol. 1.
Joshua, Essaka, *Pygmalion and Galatea: The History of a Narrative in English Literature* (Aldershot: Ashgate 2001).
Klindienst Joplin, Patricia, 'The Voice of the Shuttle is Ours', *Stanford Literature Review* 1.1. (1984), pp. 25-53.
Liveley, Genevieve, 'Reading Resistance in Ovid's *Metamorphoses*', in Hardie (1999), pp. 197-213.
Lyne, Raphael, *Ovid's Changing Worlds: English Metamorphoses, 1567-1632* (Oxford: Oxford University Press 2001).
Macfie, Pamela Royston, 'Ovid, Arachne, and the Poetics of Paradise', in *The Poetry of Allusion: Ovid and Virgil in Dante's Commedia*, edited by Rachel Jacoff and Jeffrey T. Schnapp (Stanford: Stanford University Press 1991).
Mack, Sara, *Ovid* (New Haven: Yale University Press 1988).
Martin, Christopher, ed., *Ovid in English* (London: Penguin 1998).
Martindale, Charles, *Ovid Renewed: Ovidian Influences on Literature and Art from the Middle Ages to the Twentieth Century* (Cambridge: Cambridge University Press 1988).

Works Cited and Consulted

Melville, A.D., *Ovid's Metamorphoses* (Oxford: Oxford University Press 1987).
Miles, Geoffrey, *Classical Mythology in English Literature: A Critical Anthology* (London & New York: Routledge 1999).
Miller, J. Hillis, *Versions of Pygmalion* (Cambridge: Harvard University Press 1990).
Ovid, *The Art of Love*, translated by J.H. Mozeley (London: Heinemann 1985).
Ovid, *Metamorphoses*, translated by F.J. Miller (London: Heinemann 1984).
Richlin, Amy, 'Reading Ovid's Rapes', in *Pornography and Representation in Greece and Rome*, edited by Amy Richlin (New York & Oxford: Oxford University Press 1992), pp. 158-79.
Sandys, George, *Ovid's Metamorphoses Englished* (Oxford 1632).
Sawday, Jonathan, 'Towards the Renaissance Computer', in *The Renaissance Computer: Knowledge Technology in the First Age of Print*, edited by Neil Rhodes and Jonathan Sawday (London & New York: Routledge 2000), pp. 29-44.
Slavitt, David, *The Metamorphoses of Ovid* (Baltimore & London: Johns Hopkins University Press 1994).
Solodow, Joseph B., *The World of Ovid's Metamorphoses* (Chapel Hill, NC: University of North Carolina Press 1988).
Terry, Philip, ed., *Ovid Metamorphosed* (London: Vintage 2001).
Vicinus, Martha, 'Lesbian History: All Theory and No Facts or All Facts and No Theory?', in *Radical History Review*, 60 (1994), pp. 57-75.
Warner, Marina, *Fantastic Metamorphoses, Other Worlds: Ways of Telling the Self* (Oxford: Oxford University Press 2002).
Wertenbaker, Timberlake, *The Love of the Nightingale; and The Grace of Mary Traverse* (London: Faber & Faber 1989).
Wheeler, Stephen M., *A Discourse of Wonders: Audience and Performance in Ovid's Metamorphoses* (Philadelphia: University of Pennsylvania Press 1999).

Ovid

Wilkinson, L.P., *Ovid Recalled* (Cambridge: Cambridge University Press 1955).
Zissos, Andrew and Gildenhard, Ingo, 'Problems of Time in *Metamorphoses* 2', in Hardie (1999), pp. 48-67.

Index

Acheloüs, 37
Adam, 52
Aesacus, 37
Aeschylus, 120-1
Alcott, Louisa M., 87
Allston, Washington, 136
Anaxarete, 14
Antinous, 132
Apuleius, 80
Ariadne, 110
Argus, 30
Atalanta, 37
Atwood, Margaret, 67, 72, 129
Austen, Jane, 24
artists, 8, 70, 105-21 passim, 123-42 passim
Augustus, 7, 13, 19, 27, 74-5, 108, 132
Adonis, 37, 80-1
Actaeon, 7, 28, 34, 67-83
Arachne, 8, 28, 41, 105-21
Aeneas, 9, 21, 108
Apollo and Daphne, 7-8, 17, 30, 42-3, 45-66, 70, 76
Andromeda, 21, 34

Bacchus, 39, 40, 88-9
Barnfield, Richard, 55
Beethoven, Ludwig van, 144
Behn, Aphra, 58, 60-2, 81-2
Belben, Rosalind, 23
Bernard of Clairvaux, 12

Bernini, Gian Lorenzo, 46
Bersuire, Pierre, 12, 52
bestiality, 79-81
Bible, 90-1
Blade Runner, 140-3
Boccaccio, Giovanni, 80
Boehrer, Thomas, 79-80
Bold, Henry, 54
Boreas, 145
Borges, Jorge Luis, 11
boundaries, 18-20
Boyce, Samuel, 103
Brome, Alexander, 76
Byatt, A.S., 79-80
Byblis, 17-18

Callimachus, 14
Callisto, 7
Carter, Elizabeth, 59
Cassandra, 55
Catullus, 11
Ceyx and Alcyone, 7, 14, 16
Charles II, 54
Chaucer, Geoffrey, 9, 31, 109, 127-8, 144
Cinyras, 128
Circe, 33
Clytemnestra, 120
Cocteau, Jean, 10
Coleridge, Samuel Taylor, 8, 119-20
Coleridge, Sara, 119-20
Cotton, Charles, 129-30

Croxall, Samuel, 95, 101
Cupid, 45, 47
Cyparissus, 112

Daedalus, 32, 105
D'Aguiar, Fred, 21-2
Dante, 9, 25, 114-5, 117
Daphne, 7-8, 17, 30, 42-3, 45-66, 70, 76
Darwin, Erasmus, 107
Deianira, 35
Denham, Sir John, 78
Diana, 26, 34, 42, 67-83
Diana, Princess of Wales, 67-8, 72
Dickens, Charles, 29
Dickinson, Emily, 63
Dido, 21, 29
Disney: *Hercules*, 26, 51
Doctor Who, 125

Echo, 17
Elizabeth I, 72
Euripides, 88-9
Europa, 36, 106, 109, 110
Eurydice, 10, 35, 52, 127
Eve, 52, 86, 104

Fenton, Elijah, 103
Finch, Anne, 103, 118-19
Fletcher, John, 78
flood, 19, 28, 38, 145
Forbes, Bryan, 137
Forbidden Planet, 11-12
Freud, Sigmund, 124
Fulton, Alice, 45, 46-7, 56, 62-3

Gascoigne, George, 93-5
genre, 14-15
gods, 23-8, 108
Goethe, Johann Wolfgang von, 9

Golden Age, 18
Golding, Arthur, 100, 111-13
Goodall, Charles, 59

Hadrian, 132
Haggard, Sir Henry Rider, 77
Hamilton, A.C., 116
Handel, George Frideric, 46
Hardy, Thomas, 28
'H.D.', 60
Heath, John, 71
Helen, 29
Hermes, 133-4
Herse, 25
Hippolytus, 96
Hitchcock, Alfred, 137-9
Hofmann and Lasdun, *After Ovid*, 21, 46, 144
Homer, 23
homosexuality, 31-2, 36, 80-3, 85-104 passim, 127, 131-6
Hopkins, John, 97
Horace, 14
Hovey, Kate, 107
Hughes, Ted, 10, 96-7, 140
humour, 24-6, 31-2, 33, 34-6, 37, 48
Hussain, Saddam, 124
Hyacinthus, 60

Icarus, 7
incest, 81, 87-104, 128
Io, 24, 30, 40, 70, 71, 119-20
Iphis and Ianthe, 31-2
Isis, 32
Itys, 41, 86, 101

Jacob, 90
James, Henry, 131-6

156

Index

Jentsch, Ernst, 124
John of Garland, 52
Jonson, Ben, 112
Julius Caesar, 9, 13, 26
Juno, 23-4, 30, 38, 108, 131-6
Jupiter, 19, 24-5, 26, 27-8, 30, 36, 38, 39, 45, 71, 109-10

Keats, John, 145
Kelly, Grace, 138
Kemble, Fanny, 124-5
Kipling, Rudyard, 14
Klindienst Joplin, Patricia, 102

Latona, 41-2
Leda, 106
Lelex, 39, 40
Levin, Ira, 137
Liveley, Genevieve, 128-9
Livia, 108
Lucian, 73-4
Lucretius, 14
Lycaon, 16, 24, 27-8, 71

Macfie, Pamela Royston, 115
Mack, Sara, 34
Marlowe, Christopher, 82, 108
Mars, 116
Marston, George, 126
Marsyas, 42-3
Marvell, Andrew, 56-7
Mary, 12, 52
Mathias, Thomas, 78-9
Matter of Life and Death, A, 25-6
Medea, 29-30
Medusa, 32, 34
men, 33-6
Mercury, 25, 30, 39

metamorphosis, 15-18, 22, 27, 32, 39-40, 56, 69, 76-7
metre, 15
Miller, J.H., 131-2
Milton, John, 86
Minerva, 32, 105-21
Moore, Thomas Sturge, 57
Motion, Andrew, 67-8, 72
Mozart, Wolfgang Amadeus, 48
Mulciber, 126
Muses, 117
Myrrha, 12, 17, 18, 128

Narcissus, 7, 15, 17, 145
Neptune, 32, 109
Nessus, 35
Nicander of Colophon, 14
Niobe, 22, 42
Nisus and Scylla, 41
Novak, Kim, 137, 138

Octavia, 108
Ocyrhoë, 145
Offenbach, Jacques, 10
Orestes, 120
Orithyia, 145
Orpheus, 10, 16, 17, 35-6, 37, 52, 127, 132, 139
Ovid, *Art of Love*, 12, 13, 19, 29, 50, 108; *Heroides*, 28-9
Ovide Moralisé, 12, 55

Paglia, Camille, 82, 83
Pan, 30
Pandion, 85
Paris, 37
Pasiphaë, 31
Peneus, 45

157

Pentheus, 39, 40-1, 88-9
Perseus, 21, 32, 34-5
Phaedra, 96
Phaëthon, 38
Philemon and Baucis, 39
Philips, Katherine, 58-9
Philomela and Procne, 8, 41, 71, 83, 85-104
Philo-Philippa, 58-9
Pierides, 117
Pirithoüs, 39
Plath, Sylvia, 65-6
Plutarch, 89
Pluto, 35
Poe, Edgar Allen, 136-7
Pomona, 9
Powell and Pressburger, 25-6
Pratchett, Terry, 25
Propoetides, 128-9
Proserpina, 35, 86, 104
Proust, Marcel, 9
Pygmalion, 8, 14, 121, 123-42, 144, 145
Pyramus and Thisbe, 10, 21, 22
Pyreneus, 34
Pyrrha and Deucalion, 15, 38
Pythagoras, 19-21, 39

race, 21-3
Rachel, 90-1
Raiders of the Lost Ark, 35
rape, 28, 32, 48-50, 58, 61-2, 67, 70, 71-2, 86, 89-90, 98-100, 103, 106, 109, 128
Richardson, Samuel, 48
Robertson, James, 130, 137
Roe, Sue, 29
Ross, Alexander, 107
Ross, Katharine, 137

Rossetti, Christina, 87
Rushdie, Salman, 10

Saint, Eve Marie, 138
Sajé, Natasha, 85, 95
Salmacis and Hermaphroditus, 33
Sandys, George, 75, 96, 101
Satan, 52-3
Sawday, Jonathan, 114
Scott, Ridley, 140-2
Scylla, 39
Semele, 25
Sexton, Anne, 63-5, 66
Shakespeare, 9, 10, 11-12, 22, 29-30, 49, 50, 65, 76-81, 110-11, 123, 126, 144
Shelley, Mary, 78, 123-4, 139-40
Shelley, Percy Bysshe, 143
Simpsons, The, 11
Sisson, Charles, 81, 130-1
Slavitt, David, 69, 126
Smith, Horace, 54-5
sources, 11, 14
Spencer, Earl, 67-8
Spenser, Edmund, 55, 72-4, 115-17
Stepford Wives, The, 137
Sterne, Laurence, 11
Stewart, James, 138
Storer, Thomas, 113
Strauss, Richard, 46
Stravinsky, Igor, 144
Straw Dogs, 48
structure, 9-10, 36-43
Stuart-Wortley, Emmeline, 113-14
style, 11-12
Swift, Jonathan, 54-5
Syrinx, 30

Tereus, 16, 71, 85-104

Index

Terry, Philip, 13, 22-3, 119
Thatcher, Margaret, 13
Theseus, 37, 39, 111
Titian, 43

Velazquez, 110
Venus, 8, 26, 37, 80-1, 108, 116, 125, 128-9, 131, 132, 138
Vertigo, 137-9
Vertumnus and Pomona, 9, 39-40
Vicinus, Martha, 85, 86
Virgil, 11, 14, 15
Vulcan, 116

Wadsworth, William, 52-3
Wertenbaker, Timberlake, 88, 90, 92, 96, 98
West, Paul, 13
West Side Story, 22
Wheatley, Phillis, 22
Williams, Tennessee, 103-4
wordplay, 74, 95, 105-6, 113-14
Wright, Mrs, 59
Wyndham, John, 42

Zissos, Andrew, 38

www.ingramcontent.com/pod-product-compliance
Ingram Content Group UK Ltd.
Pitfield, Milton Keynes, MK11 3LW, UK
UKHW021902220326
469204UK00008B/124